HOW
TO FIND
HAPPINESS

HOW TO FIND HAPPINESS

A Simple
Yet Comprehensive Treatment
of Christian Prayer

BARTHOLOMEW GOTTEMOLLER

Our Sunday Visitor, Inc.
Huntington, Indiana 46750

Nihil Obstat:
Rev. Robert Servatius
Censor Deputatus

Imprimatur:
✝Joseph Lennox Federal
Bishop of Salt Lake City
June 4, 1979

ISBN: 0-87973-529-5
Library of Congress Catalog Card Number: 79-88324

Published, printed, and bound in the
United States of America

529

CONTENTS

Preface 7

    ☐ Happiness: Our Goal

    ☐ Prayer: The Road to Happiness

    ☐ What Prayer Is

    ☐ What This Book Gives You

    ☐ Growing in Christian Prayer

1 / An Explanation of Mental Prayer 15

    ☐ Preamble on Vocal Prayer

    ☐ Nature of Mental Prayer

    ☐ Three Stages in Mental Prayer

    ☐ Procedure in Prayer

    ☐ Summary

    ☐ Adaptation of Eastern Prayer

    ☐ Difficulties

    ☐ Importance of Prayer

2 / Helpful Images of God for Prayer 51

    ☐ Knowing God

    ☐ God as Our Maker

    ☐ God as Our Maker in Prayer

    ☐ God as Our Father

    ☐ God as Our Father in Prayer

☐ God as Our Spouse
☐ God as Our Spouse in Prayer
☐ God as Our Life
☐ God as Our Life in Prayer
☐ Relation of Knowledge and Affections in Prayer
☐ Variety of Ways

3 / **The Contemplative Life** 139

☐ What Is Contemplation?
☐ God's Plan in Creating
☐ Three Lives in Us
☐ Perfection of the Christian Life
☐ The Two Nights in General
☐ Active Night of the Senses
☐ Passive Night of the Senses
☐ Period Between the Nights of Sense and Spirit
☐ Active Night of the Spirit
☐ Passive Night of the Spirit
☐ The Two Ways
☐ Which Is More Sanctifying?
☐ Conclusion

Preface

Happiness: Our Goal

All men seek happiness. The problem is:
Where and in what is that happiness to be
found? The answer is known, but it is difficult
to convince people to accept it. The search for
happiness is something personal to each man.
However, following the allurement of his
senses and his pride man thinks he knows
what gives him happiness. Man does know
what gives him immediate and passing happiness, but seldom what gives him perfect and
lasting happiness. Generally, it is only after
his immediate goals have failed that he is
ready to look for a deeper answer.

With a little reflection it should be evident that man's true and perfect happiness

must consist in some mutual knowing and loving such as exists between mother and child, husband and wife, friend and friend. People are our greatest joy even as they are our greatest sorrow when we lose them. The reason for this is that man, by his rational faculties of intellect and will, has a desire and a capacity to know and to be known, to love and to be loved which actually reaches for the infinite. Such a mutual exchange is only possible with another person having the same capacities and, in all its fullness, only with God.

The mutual sharing found in human love can give us a beginning of happiness, for we can share in a limited way our own being and goodness with another human person. However, if man is to find perfect happiness, it can only be through a union of mutual knowledge and love with a person who is infinite in being and goodness, namely, with God. For example, a girl can become a queen only by marrying a king. In his love he gives all he is and has to her, and she in turn gives it all back to him enriched by her personal love. Such a union of friendship with God is man's true and only perfect happiness. As St. Augustine has said, "You have made us for yourself, O Lord, and our hearts are restless till they rest in you."

Living a life of friendship with God is man's highest happiness; the deeper the friendship the greater the happiness. That is why the saints were the happiest of people. However, true friendship with God in this life can only exist in an experiential way through prayer, that is, through a personal communing with God in faith according to the reality of who he is and who we are. Without this there can be neither conscious contact with God nor, therefore, a relationship. All the happiness we find in creatures is but a sample of that which can be found in God.

What Prayer Is

Not everything called prayer is really prayer. Much of it is only a preamble to prayer. This is especially true of many Eastern forms or techniques of prayer. They are helpful toward achieving a certain self-discipline, a peace and calm of soul, a detachment from creatures, all of which are necessary and prepare the way to prayer. However, they are not prayer and may not even lead to prayer since they can stop at self. Christian prayer is

9

essentially the establishment of a relationship with God, a friendship, an I-Thou relationship based on the reality of who God is and who we are. It consists in knowing God and ourselves ever more perfectly and in living a mutual relation with him in the light of this knowledge. Hence, prayer is not just knowing and loving, but also a living. That is why the reality and the quality of one's prayer is best known from the way one lives his life. "You will know them by their fruits" (Matthew 7:16).

What This Book Gives You

This book consists of three chapters, originally separate articles, and presents a simple but comprehensive view of all Christian prayer. All forms of Christian prayer can be classified in the following way:

Vocal prayer { Private
Public (liturgy)

Meditative prayer { Meditation
Affective prayer
Prayer of simplicity

Contemplative prayer { Spiritual
Mystical

I will have little to say about vocal prayer since it is generally well enough understood, and my main purpose is to help those interested in coming to a life of personal communion with God through meditative prayer. Hence, I have only a short preamble on vocal prayer in Chapter 1. My objective in this chapter is to give a clear explanation of all that pertains to meditative prayer: its makeup, the three stages through which it progresses, and some of the difficulties one usually experiences in it.

Chapter 2 is mainly concerned with developing a deep understanding of who God is and who we are, a knowledge which is so essential for a true relationship with God. This is done by considering God under the four images of Maker, Father, Spouse, and Life.

Chapter 3 treats of contemplative prayer. The aim here is to show how one develops in a life of prayer by passing through the two purgations of which St. John of the Cross speaks and how this flowers out into one of two kinds of contemplation: spiritual or mystical.

Growing in Christian Prayer

Prayer and a life of prayer are not exactly the same thing, although all prayer should tend to a life of prayer in keeping with those words of our Lord, "Pray always." Most Christians pray on various occasions, but a life of prayer brings our relationship with God into the whole day.

The celebrated mystic, Padre Pio, had a very practical way of progressively leading others to this goal. His first requirement was that they keep the commandments of God and the Church. This, he said, is all that is necessary in order to be saved. For those wanting to do more he offered prayer, mostly vocal. This he insisted should involve both heart and mind and indeed one's whole soul. Prayer should thus not be a shutting-off of the mind as in Yoga and other Eastern forms of prayer.

To help them pray in this way with their whole soul, Padre Pio insisted that they go to Mass and holy communion daily, if at all possible, and that they should say the rosary and no doubt other Christian prayers such as morning and evening and meal prayers.

When, after this, they wanted to do still more he offered them meditation. He asked that they spend a half hour daily in reflecting on the truths of faith. If they did this they would soon find that they needed more time for prayer. In this way they would gradually enter into a life of prayer.

It is with such prayer that this book is concerned, and its purpose is not only to help those already trying to practice this kind of prayer, but also to inspire others to enter into it and to lead all to a life of prayer, even to contemplation.

CHAPTER 1

"My Lord and My God"

An Explanation of Mental Prayer

The importance of prayer cannot be exaggerated. We need prayer as much as we need God himself, for prayer is the only door that gives us conscious entrance into the world of the spirit where God dwells. Without prayer, for all practical purposes, we live in the world of sense, regardless of our intentions or protestations to the contrary. We may say that we are living for God, that our work is our prayer, that we find God in all his creatures, but these are only empty words. The impact of the sensible world is so great, and that of the spiritual or supernatural so weak, that without some time given regularly to prayer, we remain motivated wholly by the sensible, whether we know it or not.

The sensible world is indeed great and marvelous, but its Maker is much more so. If then, we find such joy in what God has made, in the beauties of nature, in entertainment, in food and drink, but especially in the association of friends and relatives, why can we not find far greater joy in God himself? Surely, he is greater than all the things he has made. But how do we find God, find him as a real and living person? The only way we can do this is to reflect on what reason and revelation tell us about his reality. Reason tells us something about God. The things he has made reveal much about him, even as a work of art reveals much about its author. Revelation gives us a still greater and more perfect knowledge of him.

Knowing God by these two means, we enter into friendship, into communion, with him by prayer. There is no other way. Now this whole process of knowing and communing with God is called mental prayer, or simply prayer. Without prayer we miss the greatest of all realities, God, who alone gives meaning and purpose to everything else.

Preamble on Vocal Prayer

Although mental prayer is our primary topic, vocal prayer is closely related to it, especially in that most important prayer: the liturgy. Then, too, vocal prayer is generally the only prayer most Christians are familiar with and not too many ever go beyond it in any conscious way. Vocal prayer, by which is understood the reading or recitation of some formula composed beforehand, may be private or public. It is private when said alone and on one's own initiative without the participation of other people. Such prayer is good and fruitful to the extent that one makes it his own, that is, wills what he is saying. Such a will is present by the very fact that one chooses to say some prayer out of reverence and love for God. Of course, the more fully his mind adverts to the prayer and his will rests in it the more fruitful it will be. However, the will to love and praise God can be present even when one does not understand what he is saying, as when one, not knowing Latin, recites the Psalms in that language.

Here, while the words are occupying his senses, his mind is or should be directed to God in a more general way in faith and love. The rosary is generally used in much the same way. Seldom does one reflect on the meaning of each Hail Mary or Our Father. These only occupy one's senses while his mind reflects on the mysteries of each decade or is simply attentive to God. It is the will that prays and not our feelings. When our feelings go along with our will, then our prayer may be very consoling, and when they do not it may be very trying; but the real value of prayer is in the will and not in the feelings. How subtly the will can be present in vocal prayer is well expressed by St. Francis de Sales when he says, "The mouth would not utter it (the prayer) if the will did not will it." Seldom therefore is vocal prayer without some value.

Vocal prayer is public when it is used by a group of people or in its name. No doubt there are various kinds of public prayer; here, however, I am only interested in the public prayer of the Church, the liturgy. Liturgical prayer is the official prayer of the Church, that is, of Christ's Mystical Body, wherein the praying faithful, who are one with Christ through baptism and the other sacraments, share in the saving activity whereby Christ brings all his members to his Father in loving obedience and worship. It is in the liturgy, "through which the work of our salvation is accomplished" (Vatican II "Constitution on the Sacred Liturgy"), that we can give ourselves in mind and will to the Father in the most perfect way. Hence, it is the greatest possible prayer, for therein we are made one with the prayer of Christ himself. It is of the liturgical gathering that those words of our Lord find their fullest meaning: "For where two or three are gathered in my name, there am I in the midst of them" (Matthew 18:20).

Christ told the apostles to preach to the whole world the salvation he had wrought for all mankind on the cross and that all who believed and were baptized would be saved (cf. Mark 16:16). It is in the liturgy, as centered around the sacraments, that we are made one with Christ and become partakers of his salvation. This is especially true of the Eucharist where we share with Christ his supreme sacrifice of himself to his Father in perfect adoration, thanksgiving, reparation, and petition. The Eucharistic celebration is the most perfect of all prayers; really, it is the one great prayer to which all other prayers (private or otherwise) must be directed in some way.

This offering, however, which we make of ourselves with Christ in the liturgical celebration of the Eucharist must be lived in our daily lives. It is here that other forms of prayer become important. The more perfectly we are united with Christ in prayer throughout the day, the more fully will we bring the power of the liturgy into our daily actions, and the more disposed we will be to enter more deeply into subsequent liturgical celebrations. All Christian prayer can help to this end, but the various forms of mental prayer are certainly the most effective. Hence, it is of these that I here wish to speak and whatever I say concerning union with Christ through such prayer should be seen in reference to Christ as present in the Church, in his Mystical Body, in the liturgy. Consider what mental prayer is, how we should go about the practice of it, what are some of the main difficulties to be encountered in it, and what is its real importance.

Nature of Mental Prayer

Mental prayer is simply a loving conversation or an affectionate dealing of the soul with God as with a real and living person. It is essentially an I-Thou relationship. Today some are inclined to disregard this. However, if prayer is not an I-Thou relationship, it is simply not prayer. I cannot pray to something: call it living history, evolution, or the ground of being. I can only pray to someone who is capable of responding. What is not a person is a thing (unless we admit pantheism), but what is merely a thing is far inferior to myself. Certainly the prayer of Christ and that which he taught to his disciples was an I-Thou relationship. Actually, the whole Bible rests on such a relationship.

Prayer then is a loving converse with God. But such a converse must be based on the reality of who God is and who we are. A child converses with its mother in one way, a husband with his wife in quite another, for the relationship is different in each case. If, then, we are to converse with God, with Jesus, it must be according to the reality of who he is and who we are. We have little difficulty in understanding our relationship with another human person, but with God it is different. Actually, we can get some very false ideas about God and ourselves. If I meet the Pope, disguised as a beggar, I will treat him as a beggar unless I know better. If I think I am a king, when I am not, I will take on airs that ill suit me. So, too, if we think we are something before God, whereas we are nothing, we will take on an attitude that ill befits a creature before his Creator.

Obtaining such knowledge is not actually prayer; however, prayer depends so much upon it that the two cannot be separated. This is especially true of mental prayer. The activity by which we seek this knowledge in mental prayer is called "making considerations." Such knowledge serves as a preliminary to prayer itself, which always consists in a loving communion of the soul with God through what are called affections. Affections are those interior acts of the will, such as adoration and love, by which we adhere to God in some way. When these are strong and sincere, they move us to bring our daily living into conformity with them. Thus, prayer gradually transforms our daily life. Otherwise, there is something wrong with our prayer.

Three Stages in Mental Prayer

Since, when starting in mental prayer, there is a greater need of knowing God and

ourselves, it is quite natural that considerations should take up a major portion of the
time given to this prayer. However, as this
need becomes less, more time is gradually
given to affections. This is as it should be. Actually, mental prayer is divided into three
stages, according to the variations existing between considerations and affections.

The first stage is called meditation. In
this stage reflections or considerations take up
most of the time, at least generally. However,
if such considerations do not end in some kind
of loving converse with God, they remain a
mere study. For this reason, other things, like
spiritual reading, the study of theology, of
Scripture, and even of other subjects can take
the place of these considerations, but never of
prayer itself. Such readings or studies, however, generally serve more as a remote preparation for prayer, since they still need to be in-
corporated into the subject of one's prayer. If
we remember that considerations are only intended to offer us matter for our loving converse with God, we will find mental prayer a
very natural and fruitful exercise.

The second stage of mental prayer is
called affective prayer. In this stage affections predominate. It is only natural that as

one's knowledge of God and of oneself grows less time should be needed before one enters into a loving converse with God. If, after a long separation, I am able to visit my mother, I do not have to think of all she has done for me before I welcome her with joy and love. All that is in the back of my head, it is a part of me. So it is with prayer. However, since we cannot experience God as we can a human person, it takes a longer time to reach that state where affections come almost spontaneously. That is why we usually have to make some short considerations before we enter into even affective prayer. This is especially so if we have come from some absorbing occupation or if we are going through a period of dryness. If we are experiencing spiritual consolations, affective prayer can indeed be very easy and natural. Even beginners in prayer may experience it at times. Once we understand this relationship between considerations and affections we should have enough prudence to know when to use considerations, and when to skip them.

Affective prayer will usually grow into the third stage of mental prayer, that of simplicity. Once there were two cardinals who were great friends. When visiting one another, they would often just sit on the veranda, happy to be together. This is a good image of the prayer of simplicity. When emotions are deep and strong words cannot express them, then just a look, an embrace, a handshake, can say far more. The Curé of Ars had in his parish a laborer who, after the day's work, always stopped for a visit to the church. One day the Curé asked him, "What do you say to Jesus?" "Oh," he said, "I don't say anything; I just look at him and he looks at me." This is the prayer of simplicity.

As should be evident, these three stages of prayer flow very naturally one from the other. However, it would be a mistake to regard them as exclusive of one another, as though, as one progressed to the higher stages, he no longer had anything to do with the lower. Actually, one may employ all three stages of prayer in the same day or even in the same period of prayer. As Dom John Chapman said, "We must pray as we can and not as we can't." If at the moment I need considerations to pray, I should use them; if I feel immediately drawn to affections or to simply looking at Jesus, I should follow this attraction. If I have a choice between them, then I should generally choose the simpler form.

Really, the simpler one's prayer the better, provided there is always some awareness or contact with God.

These three divisions are the only ones that exist in mental prayer (whether we call them by the same name or not) before we come to the so-called passive or mystical prayer, which actually begins with what is called the night of the senses.

Procedure in Prayer

What about the practice of mental prayer? Well, here the first thing is to be convinced of its need and value. If I am really convinced that prayer is the only means by which I can find God and give meaning and purpose to my life, I will be as faithful to daily mental prayer as I am to getting in my daily meals. Hence, if one misses his usual time of prayer, he will make it up the first chance he gets just as he does a meal. How long should it be? Certainly one should aim eventually at spending twenty to thirty minutes at it daily, even if he may have to start with only ten or fifteen minutes. When and where to make it is also something to be decided. Any quiet place will do. Of course, the best place is in church, but one's room or even a quiet garden or yard could do. Early in the morning is usually the best time, as this helps to give a spiritual orientation to one's whole day. However, any time one can regularly count on will do. In any case, one should have other moments during the day, like possible visits to the Blessed Sacrament, when he can turn to God and renew with him the friendly contact he has had in his mental prayer. God is a reality at all times and not just at the time of one's prayer.

Presence of God — When we come to mental prayer itself, the first thing is to place ourselves in the presence of God, to remind ourselves that God is really present as a loving and personal friend. Prayer is someone, not something. No doubt there are various ways of recalling God's presence. If one is before the Blessed Sacrament, it is quite natural to see Christ as present in the tabernacle. One may also reflect that God is present to all things by the fact that he is giving them existence, or by his grace through which he abides in the soul as a lover in his beloved. A good way of making God's presence real to us is to reflect, "If I am here, the one who made me is also here." Actually, he is more real than we are, for it is of his very nature to exist, whereas we exist only by his will. We may further reflect that, if he made us, he also made everything around us: the sun, the flowers, the trees, all the other human persons we know and love. Do we not have something to say to him? Are we not drawn to thank him, to love and admire him? Thus, right here at the very beginning of our prayer we can enter into affections.

Considerations — Being now with God and desiring to know and love him better, we proceed to reflect on some truth about him: some aspect of creation, of the life of Christ, of the glories that God is preparing for us in heaven. Generally, it is good to choose the subject of one's considerations beforehand lest we waste time getting started.

If we want to know more about God as our Creator, we can take a thing as simple as a flower. Looking at it we perceive its delicate structure, its perfection, its beauty, even the sweetness of its aroma. All this tells us something about the power, wisdom, and goodness of God who made it, made it just to give me a little passing pleasure. Do we not want to say something to him, to thank him, to admire him, to love him? If we reflect that he made us, made our hands, our eyes, our mind with its powers of knowing and loving, surely we will have much more to say to him. What would it be like to see the marvels of God as revealed in every branch of science?

Perhaps we would like to know ourselves better by reflecting on the ingratitude of sin. Here we can look at sin as the action of a child who refused to obey its mother, even tries to hit or kill her. Is not that what we try to do to God by sin? And yet in spite of such ingratitude, we see God becoming man and dying on the cross to save us from the consequences of our sins committed against himself. Who can fathom such love, such goodness? He loves me even when I have shown myself most unworthy of his love. Surely, this must move me to many loving affections. It tells me so much about God and about myself.

This quest of knowing who God is (an abyss of goodness) and who we are (an abyss of misery) can go on without end. Indeed, everything that any creature could be to us, God is this and much more. If we could understand all that God is to us under the images alone of Maker, Father, Spouse, and Life, we would come to a very deep understanding of God. All that is implied in these four comparisons is so vast and marvelous that we will never exhaust what they contain.

The end and purpose of considerations should now be clear. They give us the knowledge necessary for love. As the philosophers say, "We cannot love what we do not know." There is still one last thing we must say about considerations. After one has practiced mental prayer for some years, he will usually find that he always comes back to the same subject, that is, to something which, in a way, sums up everything that God is to him. This is as it should be, and is very much in keeping with the simplicity that should grow as we approach nearer to God.

Affections — These, as we have seen, should intermingle with considerations in our prayer. However, after spending some time in considerations, mixed with affections, it is good to give a part of one's time of prayer exclusively to affections. This will keep us from neglecting this most important part of prayer, especially when we are very distracted or dry. In choosing such affections, it is quite natural to enlarge on those arising from our preceding considerations. However, it is also commendable to have certain fixed or predetermined affections.

If one prepares the subject of his prayer beforehand, these affections can be specially chosen for the occasion. But they may also always be the same. A good set of such affections are those called the four ends of sacrifice: adoration, thanksgiving, reparation, and petition. These sum up all the basic duties of a creature toward his Creator. In adoration we acknowledge God's supreme dominion as our Lord and Maker. In thanksgiving we thank God for all the blessings we have received in both nature and grace, of which he is the supreme source. In reparation we ask pardon for our sins and seek to repair our lack of love therein. In petition we ask for all the help which only he can give. The great advantage of such a fixed set of affections is that they can be used after any subject of meditation, especially when, because of dryness, etc., we have done little in the way of considerations.

Resolutions and Petitions — Mental prayer should end in some kind of resolution and final petitions. If we have come to know God and ourselves better, and have been drawn to love him, we will want to give expression to that love in our daily life. Hence, every mental prayer should intensify this general resolve. However, if during one's prayer, he clearly sees some point wherein he is failing, it is only in accordance with true sincerity

31

to make a particular resolve on that point. Prayer should have a real effect on one's daily life, otherwise there is something basically wrong with it. We cannot come to know God and our own relationship with him, in a personal way, without a profound effect being produced in our daily living.

After our resolve to give ourselves to God, it is only natural that we should ask his help and grace. If we have really come to know him and ourselves, this need will be manifest. The prayer of petition is very beautiful when rightly understood. A father delights to give everything to his child, for he is all abundance; the child delights to receive everything from his father, for he is all need. It is this reality which creates that beautiful relationship of simple dependence and loving care that exists between them. It is true God gives us many gifts without our asking, but he wishes that we ask for others that we might realize better his love and care for us.

When praying thus for our own needs it is only natural that we think also of others. Hence, adding petitions for our dear ones and for all whom we know are in need, is very fitting. We should avoid, however, letting such petitions become too numerous or burdensome. If that should happen, we must know how to simplify them.

Summary

Once we come to see prayer as a loving converse and an affectionate dealing with God, prayer becomes quite simple, and we easily understand the various methods proposed in books on prayer. These will always contain the basic elements we have mentioned and now wish to summarize:

1. *Preparation* — Here we recall God's presence as a person who is really with us. We may also make some initial acts of adoration, humility, petitions, etc.
2. *Considerations* — Here we reflect on some truth about God or about ourselves, in order to know how we should go to him as the loving person he really is to us.
3. *Affections* — These are the real prayer, namely, acts of adoration, love, gratitude, confidence, sorrow, praise, etc. They spring from the knowledge of who God is and who we are.
4. *Resolutions and Petitions* — These are

the fruits of prayer. First, the determination to seek God as our greatest and only true good. Then, knowing that he is the source of every good, we petition him for all our many needs.

These elements should have a place in every mental prayer. Indeed, if we have a correct idea of such prayer, they will practically take care of themselves. Although one is always free to use some fixed method, as given in many books on prayer, still he should be careful never to get tied down to the method; otherwise, he will be hampered in his freedom. Actually, we should go to God as we are at the moment, just as a child goes to its mother according to the joy or pain it is experiencing. Hence, St. Bernard of Clairvaux says, "If you cannot make an act of love, then make an act of humility." That is, if you are so dry and helpless that you cannot stir up any conscious act of love, then humble yourself, making acts of humility, submission, patience, abandonment, trust. There is no state in which we may find ourselves that we cannot turn to God in prayer. If we thus learn to live our relationship with God at each moment of the day, we will come to live a life of continual prayer.

This last section presented the essentials of mental prayer. In recent years interest has grown in Eastern ways or forms of prayer, such as, Yoga, Zen, and transcendental meditation, wherein one withdraws his faculties from all considerations, or just centers his mind on one simple intelligible or unintelligible word or concept. Those who have used these ways of prayer and found them helpful may wonder if they can be used in a Christian context.

Although ways or forms of prayer similar to these are known to Christians in the West, still they have generally been recommended only in connection with states of contemplative prayer. Such is the prayer recommended in the *Cloud of the Unknowing*. The Jesus prayer is another example, although it is generally used by beginners more in the way of a repeated formula, which is called an aspiration. Eastern ways of prayer can be employed in the Christian context provided a few changes are kept in mind.

For a Christian the final goal will be quite different from that of Eastern prayer. Although the ends of relaxation, inner peace, and detachment are still valid goals, that of a self-achieved enlightenment is not. In Christian prayer this must be replaced by the goal of a personal union of friendship with God in faith. There is no place here for the total emptying of the mind of all thoughts, but only of voiding the mind of all particular concepts and of centering it on God or Christ as known by faith alone. This agrees very well with what St. John of the Cross says about voiding and purifying one's spiritual faculties by setting them in darkness concerning all things save God as known through the three theological virtues of faith, hope, and charity, which alone can unite us with God as he is in himself. A mantra or koan can be used as a help in voiding the mind of all that is not God, but it should be Christian in form, being based on some reality of faith. Also, since this kind of prayer has little in the way of considerations whereby one can grow in the Christian knowledge of God and self, this must be supplied at other times, at least by beginners, through some type of study or reflective reading on the word of God. Otherwise, one may end up more a Buddhist than a Christian. When considerations are thus supplied, beginners can use these forms of prayer with profit, for all the other essentials of mental prayer will be present, but in a more subtle way.

As a practical procedure for this kind of prayer, I would suggest the following: Since prayer is essentially a loving relationship with God based on the reality of who God is and who we are, the mantra chosen should bring out a truth stressing both sides of this relationship. Examples of such mantras would be: I poor, Jesus rich; I weak, Jesus strong; I sinner, Jesus Savior; I sad, Jesus joy; I troubled, Jesus peace. There is no end of such mantras that can be formed to fit one's need at the moment.

If one wishes to synchronize the repetition of such a mantra with his breathing so as to help integrate mind and body, he could do this either by saying the first half while breathing in and the second half while breathing out or by saying both parts while breathing out in two successive breaths. Near the end of the time given to such prayer it would be good for beginners to give some time to making certain fixed affections, such as those related to the four ends of sacrifice mentioned before. Adding some petitions and a resolution would also be good. However, all these elements are indeed present in the prayer itself though in a more implied way. Considerations are present to some extent when the mantra expresses a Christian truth. Affections are present, but they are more sensed than expressed. For example, when saying, "I weak, Jesus strong," one is really resting in the affections of humility and confidence and also in love which these affections imply. Resolutions and petitions are present by the fact that through this prayer one is moved to desire to live more fully for God and is given a sense of his need for God's help.

Prayer modeled after such Eastern forms has one advantage in that, being more passive, it is better adapted to lead one to contemplation. It is a form of prayer that can also be used, according to the need or attraction of the moment, by anyone who normally uses a more traditional form of mental prayer. Here we have a good example of how the essentials of mental prayer, once one has a clear understanding of them, can be adjusted to fit different forms of mental prayer.

Difficulties

Prayer has its difficulties indeed, but these become problems only when we fail to understand the true nature of prayer. Basically they all spring from the fact that God is not perceptible to our senses. The two main difficulties I would like to consider here are distractions and dryness.

We cannot avoid distractions in prayer. These arise from the innate weakness of our mind which cannot keep its attention fixed for long. However, just because distractions spring from a weakness of the mind they need not be willed. In other words, distractions can be present without being willed, even as we can be sick without willing it. Hence, we must often suffer distractions as we would any sickness or inconvenience. It is true, distractions can be willful, and then there is a lack of reverence for God. It is as though, while speaking to someone, we deliberately turn our attention to other things of less importance.

But how can one be sure that distractions are not willful? The best sign is when, on becoming fully aware of the distraction, one is displeased and brings his mind back to God. We cannot be responsible for a distraction until we clearly recognize it. If one spent the whole time of prayer simply bringing his mind back from distractions, he would be making just so many acts of love. The mind goes off without our willing it, but when we bring it back this is a positive choice, and therefore an act of love. Such a period of prayer might appear useless to us, but not to God. He sees the attachment of the will and also the humility we have had to practice. It is not the prayer that gives us the most light and spiritual consolation that is the best, but the one requiring the greatest renunciation of ourselves in order to please God. Distractions do just that.

Dryness is another difficulty unavoidable in prayer. It may arise from three sources: from spiritual negligence, from some physical indisposition, from the action of God. If we are refusing God something, or if we are giving our hearts too much to creatures, it is only to be expected that the things of God will have little attraction for us. The remedy is to realize that, if we seek first the kingdom of God, all the rest will be added to us. Dryness may also come from some indisposition. The mind does not function well when we are feeling ill. In this case we must be patient and go to God just as we are by some simpler form of prayer till we can remedy the trouble.

It is the dryness that arises from the action of God that especially concerns us here. This kind is a problem because we find it hard to distinguish it from that which arises from our own fault. It is true we are never free of all faults; still it is not just any fault that gives rise to spiritual dryness. It is only those wherein we knowingly refuse God something. If we cannot, therefore, lay our finger on any such deliberate refusal, we can be sure that our dryness is due, not to any fault on our part, but to God's action.

Why does God send us dryness? For our good; because he sees that it can make us grow spiritually. When the soul first enters the spiritual life, God usually draws it to himself and away from creatures by spiritual consolations. Such consolations are more pure and give a far deeper satisfaction than any sense pleasure. But, if the soul always experienced such consolations, it would go to prayer for the joy it received therein rather than out of love for God himself. True love is seen when one is willing to serve the beloved and do his will just for the joy of pleasing him even though at a sacrifice to oneself. That is why some would-be generous souls, seeing this, are inclined to ask God not to give them consolations. There is a danger of pride here. God knows better than we what we need. We should allow him to choose what he knows is best. As I have mentioned, God uses dryness to draw us to a purer and stronger love. Generally such dryness is of short duration at first, but as we become stronger in faith and love it normally becomes more protracted and frequent until we pass into what is called by St. John of the Cross the night of the senses.

Dryness also teaches us the truth of humility. It makes us realize that prayer or holiness is not so much our work as God's gift. That we attributed much of our former consolations to our own doings is quite evident from the fact that we now tend to blame ourselves for our present dryness. We must learn to realize that it is not what we do that is most important in the spiritual life, but what we freely allow God to do in us. If we attain holiness, it will only be due to the fact that it was all God's work and that our part consisted in simply accepting and in not resisting his action.

How should we act in time of dryness? First of all, we must remind ourselves that nothing has really changed in our relationship with God. Just because we feel different does not mean that the reality itself has changed. This reality we can know only through reason and faith, not through feelings. If we long for God just as much now as we did before, and if we are not knowingly refusing him anything, we can be sure that our relationship with him has not changed in the least. We should above all be careful not to give up prayer. We will be tempted to do so: (1) because we no longer find any perceptible joy in it, and (2) because we will feel that we are wasting our time, that we could be doing something better. To drop prayer for the first reason would be pure selfishness; for the second it would be from a deceptive sense of values.

Nothing is greater than loving and honoring God. By giving our time to prayer, especially when it seems to be useless, we are telling God that he has a right to our time before all else. This is an act of faith and love that greatly honors God. Finally, we should be careful never to strain, as if our lack of consolation came from the fact that we are not making a sufficient effort. God never wills that we should strain. This comes from giving too much importance to our own activity. We should, therefore, in time of dryness learn to simplify our prayer even if involuntary distractions increase. To use a book can be a way of doing this, but we must be careful to pause at times to make some affections, otherwise it will end up being merely a spiritual reading.

We may also try saying some vocal prayer very slowly, as the Our Father, the Hail Mary, or the Creed. Also repeating an ejaculation, resting between times in its sentiments, can be very good. Prayer is God's gift, but it is a gift he often gives on the ruins of our human efforts. Thus, we are made to understand that the spiritual life is God's work more than ours.

Importance of Prayer

As I have said, the importance of prayer cannot be exaggerated. If we are convinced of this, we will never neglect it. Without prayer we cannot rise above the sensible things of this life. Hence, a theoretical knowledge of God, of the supernatural, is not sufficient. This should be evident from the many theologians who in recent years have left the Church, thus acting contrary to practically all that they held and believed before. It is only prayer that can make the supernatural real and living. Without prayer we may live, "*With* faith, but not *by* faith." Prayer can and should in time make the things of faith as real and as certain as are the things of sense.

Man has to love something higher than the material things of this world. That is why, as Harvey Cox has shown in his book *Feast of Fools*, man needs fantasy. The limited things of matter can never satisfy man. He needs something more, which fantasy and fiction appear to give. What man is really seeking therein is God, the Infinite. God is the reality that fantasy is trying to attain. That is why those who live a deep life of prayer have little desire or need for fantasy or fictional reading. They have found the true reality which fantasy can never fully give.

Prayer is also necessary if we are to find truth. Truth is the object of the intellect. It would seem, therefore, that we should be able to come to it without prayer. But this is not so. Being moved by sensible desires and passions, man's intellect is easily biased by his will and so he is led into error. Only prayer can win the light and grace needed to avoid or correct this. Then, too, truth is not something; it is Someone. It is a living Person; it is God. We cannot find God and become one with him, and therefore with truth, except through prayer. That is why a mere intellectual approach to truth will never suffice. If truth is to be found anywhere as an intellectual statement, it will be in the dogmas of the Church. Without prayer these remain just statements, having no vital influence on our daily living. It is only when we have found Christ as a living person, he who has said of himself, "I am the Truth," that these dogmas become living and real, flooding everything else with light and meaning. But Christ can be found as a living person only through prayer.

Prayer is even more important in that by it alone do we attain our end. Man tends to seek his end, happiness, through various human activities. But as Christ said to Martha, "Only one thing is really necessary": to sit at the feet of Jesus so as to find everything in him. Someone has said, "It is sufficient to be"; that is, we attain our end when we arrive at that state of being or perfection intended by our Creator. The sun, a stone, a tree: all have a certain perfection or goodness proper to their natures. When they attain this, they share their goodness with others just by being what they are. If the sun were not so bright, the tree so straight, or the stone so hard, their service would be imperfect. Man, too, was made for a certain perfection. When he attains this, he automatically fulfills the end or goal intended by his Creator. Since God made man a free person, his perfection consists in freely recognizing and accepting that relationship which he has with God, and, by reason of this, with all other persons and things.

The reality of this relationship is like that existing between a child and its parents. A child's perfection or well-being consists in freely accepting to receive all that it needs in loving dependence on the care of its parents and in being perfectly submissive to their higher wisdom and goals. Man's perfection, in like manner, consists in freely accepting to find in God all that he needs, and in perfect submission to God's higher wisdom and plans. When man arrives at this state of truth and rectitude of will, he attains that perfection for which he was made. Hence, God can now use him without hindrance in his supreme designs. This design of God is directed not only to his own greater glory, but also to the highest good of the individual himself and to all other men. "It is sufficient to be." Now it is only prayer that can give us this knowledge of our relationship with God and move us to freely place ourselves wholly into his loving hands. Without prayer we live for self, having a false idea of our own independence and abilities. Thus, we fail in that docility to God which is our only task.

Prayer has one last value, one which in a way excels all the rest. As St. Teresa of Avila has said, "He who perseveres in prayer will never be lost." It is not difficult to understand why. No one who daily converses with God in prayer can deliberately plan to do something gravely sinful and stay in that state. He may, indeed, fall into some passing sin, but he will not remain in that state. The clash between remaining in sin and facing God in prayer would be unbearable. If, therefore, he always chooses to be faithful to prayer, his salvation is assured.

Prayer is the only door to reality: to the reality of God, to the reality of ourselves. Without prayer we walk in darkness, for we walk without God who is the "Light." If in the past one gave up prayer and now wishes to take it up again, he must not be discouraged if God does not at first seem to respond to his good intentions. God may wish to test his faith and love. Indeed, one will seldom find the consolations of former days. However, if one perseveres therein, he will soon arrive at that joy and peace which comes from knowing that he is doing what is right and good. In time God will show his face and say, "Behold, here I am."

Without prayer we live on the fringe of the supernatural. Like Moses we look at the promised land from afar, but never enter into it. If the true spiritual renewal, desired by Vatican II, is to be achieved in the Church, it will only be when her children have learned to enter into this promised land through prayer. There is no other gate.

CHAPTER 2

"My God and My All"

Helpful Images of God for Prayer

Prayer is a loving converse and an affectionate union of a human person with God. Now, every converse depends on the relationship of the persons involved. Since our relationship with God is something unique, for he is our Creator, it carries with it a certain totality well beyond our full comprehension. Actually, God is the source of every other relationship in our lives, so that in some way, all others are embraced in our relationship with him.

In the successful living of a relationship it is essential that the persons involved have a clear understanding of who and what they are to one another. If an employee thinks and acts as though he were the boss, he will soon be without a job. Of course, in our relationship with God there can be no doubt about his understanding, but there can be about ours both as to God and ourselves. God is an abyss of goodness, we an abyss of emptiness. We will never fully understand the reality of either, but we can always grow therein.

Knowing God

In our present state, our knowledge of God is very limited and mostly indirect. We know God only by analogy, through what he has made and through what he has told us of himself in revelation. It is somewhat like knowing an artist through his paintings and his autobiography, but never as a living person. Creation tells us much about God, for whatever beauty, power, and goodness we find in creatures, we know these qualities must exist in God in some higher way. If a creature, a fellow human being, can be to us a rock, a fortress, a physician, a father, a spouse, God must be these and infinitely more. Although revelation tells us more about God, even something of what he is in himself, still, since this knowledge can only be conveyed to us through concepts, it too is only indirect. It is only when we begin with such knowledge to live a life of friendship with God through prayer that we come to know and experience him as a real and living person.

Since it is only through created images or ideas that we can know God, it is natural for us to try and find those images which are most effective in revealing this. We find four that are outstanding: they are the images of Creator, Father, Spouse, and Life. The main value of these images is their ability to express that person-to-person relationship which is so essential in our approach to God. They also have a capacity to reveal something of the vastness of God's goodness and love in a way that can leave us in awe and wonder at what the full reality must be.

If we are to know God after the likeness of these images, prayer is essential. We cannot come to a true understanding of such relationships unless they are lived and experienced, and with God this is only possible through prayer. Mere theory will not suffice.

Hence, prayer must not be divorced from daily living. In prayer we come to know God and ourselves. This knowledge must then be put into practice in one's daily life, even as the theory of a skill must be exercised if one is to become proficient. Theory and practice must go together. In prayer we come to know something of God and ourselves. This we strive to live in our daily lives. When we run into problems and difficulties, we return to prayer to find the solution, so as to live the next day more perfectly. Thus, prayer and living go together.

Knowing God in theory is like knowing God from afar, like Moses looking at the promised land, but never entering into it himself. An understanding of God through the four images mentioned above will enable us to see the beauty of this promised land from afar, but we must enter into it through prayer so as to come to a deep and living experience of the ineffable beauty and goodness of God himself.

God as Our Maker

To see God as our Maker or Creator is quite easy. It is perhaps the basic concept most people have of him. However, all the goodness and love implied in that concept is not so apparent. The act of creation is indeed beyond our understanding even as is God himself, but it is the only explanation that makes sense for our own existence and everything around us. The fact that God has given us the power to be makers in a limited way helps us understand something of our relationship with him as our Creator. Thus, the relationship that exists between an artist and his masterpiece, a worker and his craft, can help us to understand something of our relationship with God as Creator. Although these are as nothing compared to our relationship with God, still they give us a beginning in knowledge to which other aspects that relate only to God may be added.

A person loves what he has made for he sees it as a part of himself: the child of his mind, and the fruit of his hands. If it is a masterpiece of art, it will reflect a beauty of concept, a sense of proportion, and a skill of expression that can tell us much about the qualities of the artist himself. One also loves his handiwork as something good which he wants to see succeed in its purpose. If any defect is found in it, he will repair and correct it without end; nor will he destroy it unless it becomes wholly useless. He also regards his work as his own property, as something that belongs to him and which must serve him in one way or another. If we can so love and cherish the things we have made, how much more must God love and care for us, his creatures.

God loves us, therefore, far more than any artist loves his masterpiece. He too sees us as a reflection of himself, of his own beauty, wisdom, goodness, and power. There is something of God himself in all of us so that he must love us as himself. He must also love us as his own property, as something that belongs to him that must serve him and reflect his glory. He therefore wants us to succeed in achieving that for which he made us and he is ready to forgive and repair without limits unto the very end so long as there is hope. Does not the creation story in Genesis show God much like an artist, standing back and looking at what he has made with great satisfaction? God looks at us with admiration, joy, and with hope. He loves us as his masterpiece.

God indeed loves his creation as any artist loves his work, but there are certain aspects of creation which are special and unique. First, we have a dependence upon God such as no craft has on its human maker. An artist can make a statue or a picture and then walk away; his work will remain without any more activity on his part. This is not so with God and his creation. An artist can so leave what he has made, for it does not depend on him for its existence, but only for its form.

We, however, and all other creatures depend on God for our very being and existence because we were created from nothing. Hence, he must hold us in existence at every moment. A stone by its very nature tends to the center of gravity. If it remains suspended in the air it can only be so because some external force is holding it up. So it is with all creation. Creatures by their very nature tend to nothingness even as a stone tends to the center of gravity. Hence, so long as we exist, it must be by God's action. He must be holding us in existence at every moment. We are like a child in the arms of its mother who stands on the brink of a deep abyss. If she should release her hold, her child would plunge into the abyss, but she will not do so because she loves her child. We are like that child in the arms of God. We exist only because he still loves us. This continuation of God's creative action is called conservation.

Tied in with conservation are two other divine activities: concurrence and providence. Because God is always holding us in existence, he must also concur with every act that we perform. This does not mean approval, but that God must give us the power to act even though he allows us freedom to determine how we will exercise that power. That is the limit of our freedom. God can withhold his concurrence in many ways. He may arrange that I do not think of something, that I fail to see something, or simply do not have the power or health to accomplish some task. He may arrange external circumstances so as to thwart my intentions or even the action itself. In all this God does not take away our freedom, but limits it.

We are free, but God is still the master of his creation, and his plan is being ultimately fulfilled in all things. It is only the internal intention of man's free will that can be in opposition to God's will and plan, and for this man himself stands fully responsible. For example, a man may choose to kill someone and actually do so. That this other should die is according to God's plan for him, for he could have prevented this action in many ways. However, the murderer stands fully responsible for this free act which was contrary to God's will for him. In this way God is guiding the whole of creation so as to achieve his final plan. This guiding action of God we call Divine Providence. Its complexities are simply infinite and beyond anything we can possibly imagine. It embraces the smallest activity of every creature, even the fall of a hair from our head. From this it should be evident that God's providence is guiding every detail of our lives and that nothing can happen to us that he does not will or permit for our good according to his plan.

This leads to another special aspect of creation: God's plan. Why did God create us? What is the final goal he seeks to achieve? It is true, as St. Paul says, "Who has known the mind of God?" We cannot fully know God's plan, but we can know something of it. We can know that God had to have a reason, for no intelligent being can act intentionally without a reason. Even when we kill time it is for a reason: for the reason that we have nothing better to do. Now God's reason for creating had to be himself in some way, for nothing else existed which could move him to create. But since

God is infinitely perfect, so that nothing can be added to him, he could not act in order to acquire something; that is impossible for God who has everything. Therefore, he could only act in order to give or share something. St. Thomas Aquinas tells us that it belongs to an imperfect agent to act in order to acquire something, but that this cannot befit God who is a most perfect agent. Therefore, he alone is supremely liberal because he acts, not for his utility, but only because of his goodness.

But how does one act out of love for himself by giving? This is so different from our normal way of acting, being imperfect agents, that we find it hard to visualize such a way of acting. However, we can find an example of this even in ourselves, in the so-called love of benevolence. In the love of benevolence one seeks the good of another person and not his own, yet he is moved to this, out of love for something else that is primarily loved which may even be himself. For example, a Sister of Charity, who spends the whole night at the side of a dying patient, is certainly seeking the patient's good and not her own, yet she is moved to this, primarily out of love for God. Or again, a boy may love a girl and really seek her good and not his own and yet he is moved to this primarily out of love for himself: not by loving her for himself, but by loving her as himself. The reason why we can love in this way, Cajetan tells us, is because when we love ourselves perfectly, we not only will what is good to us, as to exist, to live, to be happy, but also what it is good for us to do. Thus, it is in willing good to another that we seek what is becoming for us to do. A professor who has a very useful knowledge can find a real joy in sharing it with others so that they too may profit thereby; or a mother can spend herself for her family simply for the joy of making others happy.

If we reflect on this we can see that such a benevolent way of acting will be proportionate to the good itself which one loves or possesses, and to his own desire to do what is befitting or good for him to do. Knowing that the good which God loves and possesses is himself and that his desire to do what is fitting for him is infinite, we can begin to surmise something of God's purpose in creating. Actually, he wants to share with us his own infinite life and happiness, that is, he wants to make us gods so far as that is possible. Now God's life and happiness consists in the mutual love of friendship that exists between the three divine Persons.

It is to a share in this that God calls us. However, since love or friendship cannot be forced, God had to make us free. But still we should remember that, in his loving providence, God is doing all he can to move us (if only we will consent) to use this freedom most fruitfully. So great is God's desire to share his life with us that he will stop at nothing in order to bring it to fulfillment. To realize this we have only to look at the helpless Baby in Bethlehem's cave, the bloody Victim on Calvary's cross and at the hidden Guest in our tabernacles.

From this consideration another truth becomes evident, namely: God loves us because he is good and not because we are. No misery, wretchedness, or sinfulness on our part can make God cease to love us. Actually the greater our misery the greater is his desire to lift us out of it, because of his longing to do good. Therefore, he cannot cease to love us; it is we who turn away from him by sin, not he from us. When we do so he waits, longing for the moment of our return, like the father of the prodigal son. Such is our Maker, such is the God who is holding us and all things in existence at this very moment. What a consolation and joy to know that we are in the loving and all-powerful arms of such a benevolent God.

Another special aspect of God's love for us as our Creator is the fact that he made us to be a reasoning being, a person. God chose each of us with a very personal choice from among millions of other possible human beings. We would still be among those millions had he not loved us in an individual, personal way. Hence, we did not get here by chance; we were loved and chosen with predilection. Once so chosen, the infinite wisdom of God's providence has taken us into his loving care. If parents, when having a child, could choose all the qualities and gifts their child was to have, how carefully they would choose each and every one of them. Well, God, our Father, has done just that. Not only has he done this, he has also chosen every circumstance of our whole life with the same exquisite love. Of course, we cannot understand the workings of his providence, but if we believe and strive to live according to our faith, we will begin to see something of his loving plan even in this life, with the joyful expectancy of its full revelation in the life to come.

Since man is the only creature on earth that God has made to be a person, it follows

63

that all the rest of the material creation has been made subservient to man in some way, for what is not a person is far below man. Hence, God's love for us is seen in all the beauties and marvels of the material universe. He made them just so we might get a glimpse of his infinite wisdom, power, and beauty. It is through knowing and contemplating God in his created works that we first come to know something of who God is and of our relationship with him. So important is this particular revelation of God that we will never fully appreciate the more direct revelation of himself in Scripture without a good knowledge of it. Without a deep sense of God's infinite majesty, wisdom, and power as manifest in creation we will not be able to fully appreciate the depths of his benevolent love and mercy as revealed in the Incarnation and in the Passion.

Let us then take a look at the marvels of God's creation. In astronomy we find a manifestation of God's power and greatness that simply overwhelms us. To us our earth seems big, even though we know that it is small compared to our sun which could contain a million earths. However, there are some stars in our galaxy which are so big that, if they came between us and the sun, they would fill in all that space and go the same distance beyond. Stars are tremendous balls of fire. How would you feel if you saw a flame shoot up a mile high or a hundred miles high? Well, on the surface of the sun some flames shoot up as high as half a million miles. What such flames are like on the still bigger stars we will probably never know, for our chances of getting a close look at them seems very remote indeed.

Our sun is ninety-three million miles from our earth, but some of the planets in our solar system are two and three billion miles from us. The nearest star, however, is four and a quarter light-years away, the distance it takes light to travel at one hundred eighty-six thousand miles a second in four and a quarter years. This star therefore is some thirty trillion miles away. A space craft going twenty thousand miles an hour would take five hundred years to reach it. The galaxy in which our planet Earth is situated is one hundred thousand light-years in diameter. The nearest other galaxy is one million light-years away from us, and yet in the vast expanse of the heavens there are billions of such galaxies, some of which are as far as ten billion light-years away.

If God is incomprehensible in the great

he is no less so in the small: in a living cell, in a molecule, in an atom. All living things are made up of tiny living cells of which there are more than sixty trillion in a normal human body. In each one of these there is more organized activity going on than among humans in our biggest cities. Each cell is a little world in itself, yet it works in perfect harmony with millions of other similar cells. Now cells are made up of many molecules and these of atoms. Molecules are so small that if a light bulb were punctured and air molecules allowed to enter it at the rate of one million a second, it would take one hundred million years to fill that bulb. The atom, as we know, is still smaller, and yet it too is made up of subatomic particles which may have parts made up of still smaller parts.

God has filled our world with marvels human science will never begin to exhaust. Indeed, is it not just as easy for God to make something with the most exquisite beauty and delicacy as to make it at all? Think of the beauty and perfection of a snowflake, a flower, a tiny insect, the human ear, eye or brain. All this beauty God has made just for us, that we might come to know and love him. If God is so marvelous in his works, what must he be like in himself? So vast is God's knowledge that he knows what every atom, even what every particle of every atom is doing at every moment in the whole universe. They could not exist if he did not know and will them. All the books in all the libraries of the world are a mere beginning of man's efforts to put in words something of what God has made and of what can be developed therefrom. At the sight of this, are we not moved to cry out with the Psalmist, "What God is like unto our God?"

Not only has God made these marvels of creation to reveal himself to us, he has also made them to serve us in many ways. This should make us most grateful. What would life be like without the abundance of things God has made? What would we do without such things as wood, paper, oil, fire, electricity, and other essentials? What if there were no other people to love us or to make the many things we daily use? How limited we would be. Could each of us make a watch, a radio, a car or even a knife? And what of those marvels that make human life richer: a sunset, a mountain, a lake, a stream? All of these speak of his love and concern for us down to details we ourselves would never dream of.

Knowledge of God is not prayer, but only a prerequisite. Prayer is the loving relationship of a person with God that arises from such knowledge. Therefore, once we know God as our Creator, we should seek to live, in the light of this knowledge, a personal and loving relationship with him. We can do this through prayer in several ways. We can reflect on various aspects of God as our Creator and then allow ourselves to be moved to offer him the loving affections of our heart. This is meditative or affective prayer. Or we can just rest in God's presence, looking at him with a loving heart and let the realities we have perceived work themselves into the depths of our being — something like one who, looking at a sunset, simply lets its beauty seep into his heart. This is contemplative prayer.

When considering God as our Maker, the first thing we realize is that he really made us, and that he loves us as something which is his very own, as something which contains and expresses his own beauty and workmanship, and hence something that is his. We also see how utterly dependent we are on him, not only for our existence and continuation in existence, but even for the power to perform the least action, so that our liberty is hemmed in by his providence which is arranging everything that happens in and around us. In our craving for independence, we might feel a certain rebellion at such restraint, but this should change to love and gratitude when we realize that this absolute power which God has over us and over everything else is directed by a love that seeks our greatest good and happiness with an infinite wisdom. Surely we are far safer in his loving hands than if we were left to our own limited knowledge and power and to the mercy of pure circumstance. No, we are in the constant loving care of one who seeks our greatest good with an infinite wisdom and power that nothing can thwart. What joy, what peace, what absolute security this should give us. The great God who rules the whole universe is directing everything for my good, for my happiness, as though I were the only one he had to love and care for. What absolute faith and confidence this should stir up in our hearts as we rest before God in prayer.

In so caring for us, God loves us just as we are, for he loves us not because we are good, but because in his love he wants to have the joy of filling us with his gifts. God only asks that we open ourselves up to receive all that he wishes to give. Indeed, the more empty and needy we are the greater his joy in filling us with blessings. We may not think of him, we may not love him; but he is ever thinking of and loving us, even if, in our blindness and self-centeredness, we refuse to acknowledge his existence. No misery on our part can make him cease to love us. Is he not the father of the prodigal son?

God is our Creator and by that very fact he is more real than we are. If we exist, if we are here, then he too must be here, for we depend on him more than a sunbeam depends on the sun. We need him for the very air we breathe, for every heartbeat, for every thought and movement. He is simply everything to us both in ourselves and in all the things around us. As St. Paul says, "In him we live and move and have our being." In prayer this should draw us to adoration, to cry out with St. Francis of Assisi, "My Lord and my God, my God and my all."

If all this seems too fantastic to be true, we have only to look at the world around us. How are we to explain the marvels of our universe which science opens up before us? Can God himself be less marvelous than what he has made? If we cannot fathom the vastness of the heavens, the activity of the atom or the workings of a living cell, how can we expect to fathom God himself? Creation is utterly beyond our comprehension. Why then should not God himself be far greater than we can ever understand? If we try to question or deny his infinite reality and power, all creation will stand up and cry out against us. What awe, what wonder, what joy and praise and gratitude should fill our hearts when at prayer we recall that God is real, more real than all the universe and that he loves us, loves us as though he had no one else to look after.

Great as creation is, it is still only a sample of God himself. If I can find such joy in creatures, in these samples, how much greater must be the joy to be found in God himself? Surely he is greater than the things he has made. Creatures are beautiful and marvelous, but they are only means, leading me to God. If I stop at them and try to make them my end, they always let me down. God is our Creator, and he has made us for himself. Hence, he alone can be our end, our happiness; as St. Augustine has said, "Our hearts are restless till they rest in him."

If God is our Creator, he is so in the likeness of a father, for he has made us persons. In the Bible the name Father is frequently applied to God, most significantly in the prayer we call the Our Father. Indeed, the father-child image well expresses that person-to-person relationship which exists between God and ourselves. Every person is essentially a relation and as such is incomplete without his corelation, another person, his other self. Thus it is that a father is incomplete without his child and a husband without his wife. This need of man for another person, for another self, is very evident in the creation story where, after creating Adam, God said, "It is not good for man to be alone," and so he made for him a helpmate, Eve.

The fact that every person is essentially a relation is true of God himself. Plato is said to have asked, "If God exists, whom does he know, whom does he love?" He saw that no person could live in isolation, not even a divine person. This is because a person, that is, an intellectual individual, has a capacity to know and to be known, to love and to be loved, and so can only find fulfillment through an interchange of such giving and receiving with another person. This interchange will vary according to the nature and condition of the persons involved. It is most perfect between those wherein the giving and receiving are more total and also more equal and complementary, as in the Trinity itself, and then to a lesser degree in the relationship between husband and wife. It is less perfect between those where this giving and receiving is less total or less equal, even though still complementary, as between father and child, master and servant.

Of course, this interchange should be in conformity with the reality of the persons involved, and its perfection, relatively speaking, will be according to that reality. Thus, the mutual interchange between father and child will have a different perfection from that which exists between husband and wife. Between father and child there is considerable inequality, for the child is in the process of becoming like to his father. Hence, the father is more giving and the child is more receiving. That is why the image of a child best expresses our relationship with God. We are like little ones in the divine life in which we must grow and become perfect even as our heavenly Father is perfect (cf. Matthew 5:48). However, in this present life we will always remain as children before God. That is why our perfection must consist in becoming ever more childlike according to those words, "Whoever humbles himself like this child, he is the greatest in the kingdom of heaven" (Matthew 18:4).

The most basic reality in the father-child relationship is that the father is abundance and the child total need. Because of this, the father desires to give everything to his child and in so doing finds a real joy and fulfillment which accords with the reality of his relationship. The child on his part desires to receive everything from his father for that accords with the reality of his relationship. He does not experience any humiliation in this; rather it is the source of all his joy and security. Thus, father and child perfectly complement and mutually fulfill each other.

In this relationship the father may seem to be all giving and the child all receiving, but there is a sense in which the child gives and the father receives. While the father gives himself as abundant, the child gives himself as emptiness. Both give themselves in a way that is mutually fulfilling. Should they try to reverse these roles, we immediately see how preposterous that would be. We can hardly imagine a father expecting his small child to provide for him, but we can picture a child, especially ourselves in relation to God, seeking to provide for ourselves without the care or need of our heavenly Father. In this we are much like a two-year-old trying to earn his own living. Imagine all the difficulties he would experience and hence the problems we have. Yet once a child comes to realize and accept his father's love and desire to care for him, what peace and joy and security is his. So it is that our well-being consists in knowing and living the truth of who God is and who we are, which is best revealed by the father-child relationship.

To better understand our relationship with God, let us consider more fully the relationship that exists between an earthly father and his child. A father loves his child as himself, as one in whom he continues his own existence. That is why, for example, a loving father wants his child to achieve everything that he himself desired, but was unable to attain. The only limits a father puts to his desires for his child are his own ambitions. Because of this identity, a child shares through love everything his father is and has. There is nothing a loving father will not spend on his child in case of need. He will even go into debt to provide medical care or the best of education for his child. Because of this, a child possesses everything his father has, but more securely than if he had it in his own keeping, for the father has greater wisdom. Also a father is never envious of his child's successes; on the contrary, he sees his child's successes as his very own. Thus, he is most ready to forgive his child even while correcting and encouraging him to the highest ideals.

Strictly speaking, a father is obliged to care for his child since he is responsible for bringing him into the world. However, because of his love, he never really thinks of it as an obligation. This is a good example of how "love is the fulfilling of the law" (Romans 13:10). If it is a joy to give to any child in need, what must this joy be when the child is one's very own? That is why a father's love or care has no limits save his own desires and ambitions. That, too, is why a father would be grieved if his child sought from others or tried to do himself something beyond his power, when his father is so anxious to help him. For this reason a loving father can never refuse his child anything that is really good for him.

To do so would be to betray the confidence his child has in him. Hence, even if he cannot give what his child actually asks, a father will always try to give him something else, even better, just to prove his goodness.

We saw before that there is also a way in which a child can be said to give. He has no talents, no power, no strength, no possessions, and even if he did, he would not know how to use them. He has only himself, weak and poor though he be; but it is just this that enables him to give that which his father desires most to receive. He can give his simple faith, his loving confidence, and that total abandonment which puts him wholly into the care of his father.

Actually, there is nothing the father desires more than this, for it contains a kind of implicit praise and honor which fills the father's heart with delight. A child's return, therefore, consists in those virtues of faith, love, confidence, abandonment, in a certain simplicity, and even in a kind of zeal that boasts about his father and wants others to know and love him even as he does. If, besides this a child is so loving and confident that he will come and tell all his faults to his father, knowing that he will thus find forgiveness and help, how can the father resist such simple and total trust?

When we consider all this in our relationship with God, how beautiful and vast it becomes. The love of all earthly fathers is but a spark compared to God's love. Moreover, if a father's love for himself is the measure of his love for his child, how great must be God's love for us. Surely, he must desire to share with us his own infinite being and happiness to the highest possible degree. In other words, he wants to make us gods insofar as that is possible. True, he cannot make us gods by nature, for then we would have to be uncreated and without beginning, which is impossible; but he can make us gods by participation, which is something far beyond our comprehension as we shall see later.

God loves us as he loves himself and so he wants to share with us all that he is and has, but in the way of a father, that is, not by putting everything into our hands, but by himself using it for us as the need arises. Hence, our part is to have a childlike confidence in God. The power, wisdom, and even the goodness of an earthly father is limited and sometimes absent, often just when most needed; but this can never happen with our heavenly Father, for he is always present and there is nothing that can resist his power nor escape his loving concern. All the arrangements of his providence are planned with infinite love down to the smallest detail. This is true of the past, the present, and also of the future. We are not at the mercy of fate, but ever in the loving arms of the best of fathers. If only our faith and confidence would equal his love and power, we would pass from one experience to another of his all-embracing care.

Our abandonment would be perfect and we would experience the truth of those words which assure us that he who trusts in the Lord will never be confounded (cf. Isaiah 49:23). Even suffering and trials would not shake our confidence, for we would cry out with Job, "Even if he kills me, yet will I trust him" (cf. Job 13:15). Our very faults would draw us closer to him as a deeper experience of his infinite goodness and love. If a little child, after having done something he knew his father did not want, would come and throw himself into his father's arms and with remorse in his eyes say, "Daddy, I'm sorry, just do with me what you think best," would his father give him a good spanking? Rather would he not give him a big hug with words such as, "Oh, yes, I forgive you, but for your own good I do not want you to do such things"?

Seeing ourselves as God's children can also give us a true understanding of humility. A small child is humble by nature; he has no idea of excelling others, and yet this does not disturb him in the least, for all his needs are perfectly cared for by his parents. It is only when one sees some value in excelling others that he can suffer humiliation. Humility is the recognition of the truth, which for a child is to see that he is nothing of himself, but that his father is everything to him. Such humility is natural to a child, and he finds therein a freedom which makes his state so wonderful and happy. So it should be with us. We should be happier that God is everything than if we had something of our own. We can never be sure of ourselves because of our limitations. But, we need never worry that God will fail us. Humility therefore is the perfect blending of two realities: the reality of who God is and who we are. If we look only at our nothingness, we will become discouraged; if we look only at God's goodness, we might become presumptuous, taking his gifts for granted. For true humility, both of these realities must be seen and lived together.

God is our Father, and as such he is all giving, but we as his children, must also give. This we do through the virtues of faith, confidence, love, abandonment, etc., which in our relationship with God should be absolute and total. Only such a complete return is proportionate to the reality of his infinite wisdom, power, and goodness. In giving ourselves to God in this way we will always find far more joy and security in him than any child could find in the most loving of parents. How could it be otherwise, seeing as Scripture says that God cares for us more than for the birds of the air and the lilies of the field? It is this childlike love, this gift of ourselves, that honors God, delights his heart, and fills our own with a joy that leads to praise and adoration. Seeing how wonderful and good God is should fire us with zeal: we should want all people to know their heavenly Father, so that they too might share in the joy and happiness we have found in his infinite goodness and loving care.

God as Our Father in Prayer

When we come before our heavenly Father in prayer, the first thing we should realize is that he is real and the very best of all fa-

81

thers. That he is real means he is here present with me at this moment with all his loving kindness. Perhaps we have known a loving and kind father in our own families; but much greater is God's fatherly love for us. To come to a deep conviction of God's reality and fatherly love, faith is essential; we have no other way. A child senses his father's loving care; he knows his father's love because he has experienced it. We cannot know our heavenly Father in this way. He is indeed loving us in everything that comes to us, but we do not feel him therein. We experience only creatures, the secondary causes. We may occasionally feel his presence through a sensible consolation at prayer or in some special grace, but such experiences are rather rare.

If we try to understand God only through such experiences, we will never really know our Father. Hence, the need of faith. God has told us that he is our Father, and, everything we can know through reason tells us the same. This we must believe and, what is more important, act on. We must be willing to step out in faith, in order to experience the reality of our Father's love. It is prayer that must give us the light and strength to do this. A child first experiences his father's love and then believes in it. We must first believe in our Father's love and then by acting on it come to experience it. The more we step out in faith the more we will come to experience our Father's loving care, and so our faith will gradually grow until it becomes a deep conviction.

What joy to know, with the deep conviction of faith, that we have a Father, infinite in wisdom, power, and goodness looking out for our every need even the very smallest. If he loves me as himself, if he wants me to be perfect even as he is perfect, what then can I not expect from him?

What joy also to know that my misery and littleness are no obstacle to his love, but rather the very reason why he loves me so much. It is my very emptiness that moves him in abundance to fill me with his gifts. All this we should dwell upon in prayer.

The one great evil I must avoid is pride, the desire to be self-sufficient. If I give way to this, God will step back; he will not force himself upon me; he loves and respects me too much for that. No, he will simply wait until I come to see my mistake and then, when I return to him like the prodigal son, all his pent-up love will break forth like a torrent. Our well-being does not lie in anything we have and can do, but only in our Father's loving care. He will always be there when needed. However, he does not always give us provisions in advance, for then we would be prone to seek our security in these things rather than in him and in his unfailing care.

We must also remember that God has no need of our talents or works; he can do everything we can and far better. However, he does need the gift of ourselves, the gift of our free will which he will not force. The only return he asks for all his love is that we give ourselves into his loving care. He will be everything to us if only we will consent to be his and this we must learn to do in prayer.

How different our days would be if we could live each one of them in the conscious presence of such a loving Father. Truly we would enjoy the freedom of the children of God, and this is what prayer should gradually effect in us. Prayer should bring us to reality, and to a living experience of it. It is not some fantasy, dream or illusion that we must live; such things may soothe our egos for the moment, but reality will always catch up with us in the end. Why go after such things when the reality is far greater than the wildest dream? What could give us greater joy, freedom, and security than to be the child of such a loving and all-powerful Father?

God as Our Spouse

In the Old Testament Israel is at times referred to as the spouse of Yahweh; in the New Testament the Church as well as the faithful Christian is often called the bride of Christ. The image of God as Spouse is not new to the reader of Scripture. Although the image of father and child may best express the reality of the essential inequality that exists between the Creator and the creature, still the image of spouse best expresses the reality of the perfect state of union to which God has deigned to raise us with himself through grace. God has effected this especially through the Incarnation of his Son. However, God raised man to a certain equality of friendship with himself even at the moment of his creation. Thus, in Genesis we see God visiting Adam in the cool of evening and speaking with him as with a friend. As we know, this state did not last long because of Adam's sin.

The friendship which Adam experienced with God was only a prototype of that more perfect friendship to which God now calls all men to himself. In Christ he calls us to a share in his own divine life. In the Godhead the Father's knowledge of himself has to be something substantial and as perfect as himself, but as other, that is, as another person, the person of his Word or Son. In their mutual knowing and being known they love one another and this love also has to be something substantial and as perfect as God himself, but as other, that is, as another person, the Holy Spirit, who is the substantial love of the Father and Son. Thus, in the Trinity we have a unity of nature with a trinity of persons that is unique. Although no human friendship can equal that of the Trinity, still it can have some likeness to it.

In Genesis it is recounted that God made man to his own image and likeness. This means that God made Adam a free person with the innate desire to know and to be known, to love and to be loved. Since Adam by nature could not be as perfect as God, his knowing and loving of himself could in no way constitute another person equal to himself. Hence, God, knowing that no person can exist in isolation, saw that it was not good for man to be alone and so he made for Adam another self, a helpmate, Eve, one like to himself.

Man's highest natural happiness and perfection therefore consists in a life of mutual friendship with his other self, that is, with another human person, especially one of the opposite sex. However, God willed to give man something more than this; he chose to call man to friendship with himself which requires man's free acceptance and a return of love. Man fulfills this in the present life through faith, whereby he merits to possess it eternally in heaven where the freedom to reject will no longer be possible.

That is why God put Adam to a test of faith. As we know, Adam and Eve, both as individuals and as human partners, failed this test and so rejected God's friendship. Nevertheless, God, in his infinite mercy and goodness, chose to make a new offer of friendship with mankind in a much higher and more perfect way. This offer of friendship was foreshadowed in Adam and prefigured in all God's dealing with Israel, but was brought to fulfillment in the gift of his divine Son through the Incarnation. Through this stupendous gift of grace, God now calls all men to a twofold friendship: one with Christ as man in a new divinized human life and the other with himself in and through Christ in the Trinity itself.

Christ, by reason of the Incarnation, possesses two natures, human and divine, and in both he is incomplete without his other self, without another person. In his human nature, as the new Adam, he is incomplete without his new spouse, his new Eve, who is all mankind, the Church, perfectly lived and exemplified in Mary. In his divine nature he is incomplete without his other self, the Father, and their mutual bond of love, the Holy Spirit. In Christ we are now called to share in both of these. We are called to share a human life of friendship with Christ in likeness and in imitation of Mary; and we are called to share in his divine life of friendship with his Father, for, forming with him the whole man we can no longer be separated from him as God's only Son. Thus, in him we are taken up into the very bosom of the Trinity.

It is therefore evident that we have a relationship with God in the likeness of a spouse. To understand something of what this implies, let us take a look at human friendship or marital love, imperfect though this may be, especially since man's fall. For human friendship or marital love St. Thomas Aquinas requires two things: the love of benevolence, and that it be mutual. He also says that it demands a certain equality, for friends either take equals or their friendship makes them equal. This is because of the equal sharing which friendship always implies. Hence, there can be no real friendship between a man and his dog, except by analogy, for they are very unequal in nature.

Friendship requires the love of benevolence. As we have seen, by the love of benevolence one seeks the good of another and not his own (even though he is moved to this, out of love for something else which is primarily loved). In true human friendship or married love, when a man loves a woman, he seeks to do everything that will please her and be good for her. In this he is certainly seeking her well-being and not his own, and yet, since he sees her as his other self, he is really loving himself in her, but in a higher way, that is, himself as existing more really and concretely in her.

His love, therefore, is not selfish. In so giving himself to her in love he is fulfilling his capacity for giving and so finds a certain fulfillment even if she should make no return of his love. However, it is only when she returns his love in the gift of herself that their union of friendship becomes mutual and so perfectly fulfilling for both of them according to their capacity of giving and receiving. Although this giving and receiving applies to both, still there is a certain order therein: the man, who is more the principle and the source, first gives and the woman receives. Only then does she give back everything in a return of love. Thus, if a king should choose to marry a poor country girl and make her his queen, all he asks of her is that she be willing to receive everything he has to give her and then return it to him enriched with her personal love. It is through such a mutual giving and receiving that spouses find a wonderful fulfillment and a power and security well beyond their personal assets. This is well expressed in that saying of the sage, "A brother helped by a brother will be like a fortified city" (cf. Proverbs 18:19). Although the effects of such a union are more easily experienced than understood, still they merit some explanation.

When a boy and girl fall in love they feel as though they could live together forever and never need another thing. Of course, this is an illusion, but it does point to what our true goal must give. What lovers really seek is unity; they want to become one, not just by sharing their gifts, for that would not remove loneliness, but by sharing themselves through these gifts. How secure a girl feels while resting in the loving strength and firm support of her husband, and how strong and self-reliant he feels when experiencing the tender esteem and loving confidence of his wife. By such a mutual sharing of themselves through their gifts they complete each other in a way that seems to exhaust all they need and desire. If in so sharing themselves they could share total being, that is, every possible good and perfection, then indeed they would experience absolute and perfect fulfillment. This, however, is possible only by such a union with God who alone is total being.

Lovers seek unity because this gives them the opportunity to share everything the other is and has. They seek this unity through a mutual knowing and a mutual giving of themselves in love, that is, in works of love. Lovers want to know each other ever more perfectly so that they may love each other more totally. That is why they want to be together, why they find such mutual joy in those intimate exchanges of confidence. They want to know the other so as to increase their unity in love. One cannot love what he does not know. Hence, the greater their knowledge of each other's goodness the greater will be their love.

But lovers also wish to express their love by doing things for each other and by working together. Because the love of benevolence seeks the other's good they want to do that which will please and make the other good and happy. It is their way of sharing their goods in unity. They also seek to work together. We desire to accomplish, to do and make things, because this gives us to know and experience what we are. Now the greatest work anyone can do is to make another self, a person equal to himself. Hence, lovers seek to give expression to that which seems to be the greatest reality in their lives, namely, their mutual love. This they do by so giving themselves to one another as to be fruitful of a child, a concrete and total expression of their mutual love. The child is a work equal to themselves in every way and hence their greatest possible work on the human level.

The nature of this union is such that certain qualities or properties flow from it. The first of these is permanence. Since their union gives them everything they desire, they want it to last forever. If not, then something essential is wanting to their love. Marital union also carries with it a certain exclusiveness. Both parties are willing to share with outsiders the goodness of their beloved even as their own goodness, but they are not willing to share their beloved in those things that would lessen their unity or mutual possession of each other. To do that would be to accept one's own diminution or destruction. As for their personal limitations and faults, if these are such as to make them more dependent on one another, then they can be a source of delight, for they increase unity and their need of each other. But if they imply a lack of confidence or love or a tendency to seek one's good elsewhere, then they are disruptive, for they weaken unity. Husband and wife may be willing to forgive such faults, but they do expect a sincere repentance and resolve not to repeat them.

Although such a union of human love and friendship is man's highest natural good, still it cannot fully satisfy him. This is because his intellectual nature has a capacity for total being and total good. By his intellect man wants to know all being and he wants to be all being. By his will he wants to possess all good and he wants to be capable of doing all good so as to be loved as all goodness. Since man does not have this in himself he can only find it in an exchange of knowing and loving with someone who is all being and all good, namely, God. Of course, this is impossible unless God takes the initiative. If a poor girl wishes to share in the riches and power of the king, she can only come to this if the king himself first loves her and asks her to be his queen. Then he shares all he has with her and she can give it back enriched with her love.

Let us now apply all this to that higher union with himself to which God calls us through grace. That which human lovers seek, but can never fully achieve, God has now made possible to us through the gift of his own divine Son. We are called to a human friendship with Christ since as man he is incomplete without us, his other self, even as Adam was incomplete without Eve. In the gift of this new divinized human life, Christ is the principle, the bridegroom, and we, all mankind, are his spouse. Both together we make up that one man, that new creature, man living by the life of God of which St. Paul speaks.

In taking us to himself, however, Christ encountered a difficulty. We, his spouse, were at enmity with his Father, bound by the slavery of sin. If he is to take us to himself and make us his spouse to share his friendship with his Father, he must deliver us from our disgrace and bondage by a great feat of love and self-sacrifice. Of course, he could not do this without our consent. This Christ actually accomplished on Calvary, not alone, but as one with all mankind willing and consenting in Mary. Mary and we in her were one with Christ in that supreme act of love and giving of himself to his Father. Adam had rejected God's friendship through pride and disobedience, preferring his own will to God's will. The reparation required to reestablish this friendship, should be an act whereby this new man would sacrifice himself totally in humble obedience to the Father's will.

That is why on Calvary Christ, and we in Mary, became obedient unto death even to the death of the cross for which cause God has exalted all mankind in Christ and given us a name in Christ that is above all other names. By this supreme act of love of the new Adam and Eve, Christ and we in Mary, man's ability to share in the divine life has become the inalienable possession of the whole human race. Mary is truly our co-redemptrix, for by her willing and consenting she fulfilled, in our place, that which we were as yet unable to perform. What she there did we must now ratify in our own life by accepting God's offer of friendship in Christ and by living with him a life of perfect obedience to his Father's will even unto death, as did Mary. This ratification we profess in baptism, but we give highest expression to it in the Mass where, with Christ, truly present in that supreme act on Calvary, we can now unite ourselves with him, as Mary did.

As we have seen, the essence of human friendship resides in the love of benevolence wherein one loves another as his better self and therefore seeks this other's good even before his own good. We have also seen that it must be mutual and demands a certain equality. In Christ, God has certainly made himself equal to us, emptying himself and becoming a man like unto us in all things but sin. Not only has he made himself our equal, he has also made himself our bridegroom, so that he is incomplete as man without us, his bride. He must love us, therefore, as his other self. Since his love cannot be otherwise than absolutely perfect, it must be so as benevolent. Hence, not only does he love us as his other self, he loves us, in a certain sense, more than himself; did he not die that we might live? That Christ loves us as his friend with the love of benevolence we cannot doubt. The difficulty or prob-

lem is with us: do we love him in return with
the love of benevolence? We have seen how
human lovers seek to make their friendship
mutual; let us, by applying this to our relationship with Christ, see how we must live a
life of loving friendship with him.

What lovers seek above all is unity. This
they achieve not merely by sharing their gifts
with each other, but by also sharing themselves through these gifts. Therein they find a
certain totality and fulfillment that seems to
exhaust their every need and desire. Since
human lovers are limited in what they have to
share in this way, they cannot find the perfect
happiness they desire. But with us and Christ
it is different: he does have the totality of
every good and all he asks is that we open ourselves in love so as to receive everything he
has to give us and then return it to him
enriched with our personal love. If a girl can
find such joy and security in the arms of her
beloved, what should we not feel in the arms
of Christ who owns and rules the universe?

As we have seen, such a union depends on
mutual knowledge and love. For mutual
knowledge some kind of presence is required
with an exchange of confidence: that free and
spontaneous revelation of oneself to each

other. We can understand the importance of presence in the case of human lovers, but how are we to come to this with Christ? How can one have a human friendship with someone who is not sensibly present? The marvel is that Christ is still sensibly present, but he is only perceptible to the eyes of faith. He said to the apostles that he was going away and coming back to them (cf. John 14:28), and again, "I am with you all always, to the close of the age" (Matthew 28:20). Christ is present in his Church and he is there still teaching, guiding, and ministering to us through the hierarchy even as he did himself while still on earth. During his earthly sojourn Christ's divinity was hidden under an individual human nature.

Now he hides both his divinity and his humanity under a social nature, the Church, and yet he is just as truly present there as he was back in Palestine; but only faith can see him now even as then. Christ is also present and active in the sacraments. In the sacrament of Penance we can fall at his feet as did Mary Magdalene and can hear his words, "Go in peace, your sins are forgiven" (Luke 7:48). At Mass we can stand at the foot of the cross and with Mary unite ourselves with Christ in his supreme gift of himself in love to the Father. In communion we can rest our head upon his breast in loving friendship as did St. John, and there commune with him in the greatest intimacy of friendship. Christ is also present in our brothers. We can take him into our homes as did Martha and Mary. We can eat at table with him, share his travels and even his ministry of teaching and healing as did the apostles. "As you did it to one of the least of these my brethren, you did it to me" (Matthew 25:40).

God knows we need sensible realities, but he also knows that true life is not found in the senses but only in the spirit. That is why he has raised his sensible presence to the level of the spirit, to the level of faith. Faith is fundamental in all our relationships with Christ and hence also in the matter of friendship. When a couple fall in love, their knowledge of each other comes through sensible contacts. Between us and Christ this must be supplied by faith, for even the sensible contact possible with Christ in the sacraments depends on faith. Even if one is first introduced to the reality of God by some soul-shaking experience, he must still turn to faith so as to know more fully the God who thus touched him. There

can be no friendship with Christ without faith
and above all faith in his personal love for us.
Christ's personal love has to be the starting
point of any friendship with him, for, if we
love Christ, it is because he has first loved us.
How much he has loved us we find in the Gospel and in the many gifts contained in creation
itself. When we step out and begin to act on
our faith, then we gradually begin to experience the reality of Christ and his love, and so
our faith grows. Faith approaches perfection
when through such experiences we become so
convinced of his love for us that nothing can
shake it and we are ready to cry out with Job,
"Even if he kills me, yet will I trust him."

Friendship requires mutual exchanges of
confidence. Between us and Christ this is ob-
tained only through prayer because we can
communicate with Christ only through
prayer. Without prayer there can be no real
friendship with Christ, for there can be no real
personal knowledge of Christ but only a mere
theoretical knowledge. If a husband and wife
are always doing things for one another, but
never sit down and share their inner thoughts
and desires, their marriage will soon break up
for lack of any deep communication. The same
is true of friendship with Christ. Work can

become prayer only when it is the overflow of prayer. If prayer has not gone before, it is an illusion to say that one's work is his prayer. As human lovers need their moments of intimate exchanges of confidence, so too we and Christ. We find these moments in the sacraments, in the liturgy, and in prayer. Prayer is no monologue, but the mutual sharing of confidence. However, since Christ is the greater one, prayer should consist more in listening than in speaking. We must learn to listen to Christ, but he speaks softly and more by a sign, a look, a touch, a thought, an event and through others. As we become more attentive to him, we will perceive what he has to say more readily. For this we need peace, silence, and detachment: true purity of heart.

Friendship also requires a mutual giving, for it is by sharing what they have and are that lovers find true fulfillment. This sharing can be on several levels. There is the level of words, where they tell each other of their love; there is the level of deeds where they do favors for one another; but especially there is the level of giving themselves. So it must be between us and Christ. We must believe that Christ loves us, that he shares all the infinite wisdom and strength of his divinity with us, and that his loving care is looking out for our every need. We, on our part, must offer him the joy and comfort of our tender esteem and loving confidence. We can be certain Christ will never let us down, but how often we let him down.

On the level of deeds lovers seek to do favors for one another to witness to their love: deeds speak louder than words. Certainly faith tells us that Christ is loving us in all the creatures he has made for us and in his providence that is arranging everything for our good. But, what of our return of love? What can we do for him? Where do we find him? What are his needs? He gives us the solution when he tells us: "What you do to one of these least of my brothers you do to me" (cf. Matthew 25:40). We can make a return of love to Christ in our neighbor. This is the greatest proof of our love for Christ since it proves the strength of our faith on which such love must rest.

Lovers also wish to work together, to give expression to that which is the greatest reality in their lives, their mutual love. If human lovers seek to give expression to their mutual love in the child, we must seek to give expression to our mutual love with Christ in forming other Christians. The bond of mutual love which unites us to Christ is the same as that which unites Christ with his Father, namely, the Holy Spirit, for the love of God has been poured into our hearts by the Holy Spirit *who* has been given to us (cf. Romans 5:5). Thus, as Christ by the Holy Spirit offered himself to his Father in an act of total love on Calvary, and Mary with him as the whole man, thus winning the salvation of all mankind, so we can now unite with Christ in giving ourselves to the Father's will and thus win the application of this salvation to other souls. We can become co-redeemers in a more limited way. Hence, we become spiritually fruitful so that those words can apply to us, "The children of her who has no husband will be more numerous than of the one who has a husband" (cf. Isaiah 54:1). It is in this way that we are united with Christ in his greatest work of love, the salvation of souls. Christ is truly a friend who shares absolutely everything he is and has with us.

As certain qualities flow from the nature of human friendship, so too from our union with Christ. Finding Christ to be everything to us, we want our union with him to last forever far more than do human lovers. They desire to deepen their union in this life, but we, while also seeking to deepen our union with Christ in this life, look forward to that far more perfect union which will be ours with him in eternity. Also, our union of friendship with Christ carries with it a certain exclusiveness. To be sure, Christ will always be faithful to us, but are we always faithful to him? Christ does not desire that we should seek our primary good and happiness in anything or anyone apart from himself. This is because his love for us is so great and he knows that we cannot find ultimate happiness in anything apart from himself. He does indeed desire that we share our gifts with others, but this must never be done in such a way as to draw us away from him as the final source of all our happiness. Even our faults and limitations he does not mind if they make us more conscious of our dependence on him; but if they show a lack of faith or love or confidence, then they grieve him deeply, for they then weaken our union with himself.

Christ is our greatest friend, our bridegroom, who shares with us all the riches that are his. But Christ is also God, and as such he is incomplete without his other self, his Father and their mutual bond the Holy Spirit.

Since we form one body, with Christ as head, and can no longer be separated from him in his human nature of which we are his fullness, his Mystical Body, we are taken up with him into his divine life in the Trinity itself. If the son of a king marries a girl, she is taken up into the royal family and so is loved by the king as one with his son. So it is, that, being one with Christ, we are taken up into the divine family of the Trinity. When the Father now knows and loves his Son and gives everything to him, he knows and loves and gives everything to us as one with his Son; and when the Son now knows and loves and gives everything back to his Father, we do all this in and with him by the Holy Spirit who is the mutual love of Father and Son. Thus, we possess eternal life even now to the extent that our will is conformed to Christ in faith and love. Hence, those words of our Lord, "He who believes in the Son has eternal life" (John 3:36). We now possess God's own life through faith, but the full experience of it we will receive only in the beatitude of heaven.

God must love us. Perhaps we can get some idea of what this implies by considering those words of Louis Evely, "When we love someone, we give him power over us." When we really love someone we cannot refuse him anything in our power that is good for him. Since God loves us, even as himself, what is there that he can refuse us? Nothing, surely. Actually, to the extent of our faith and confidence in Christ we can lay claim to the very omnipotence of God himself. God cannot refuse us anything that is good for us. We are, in effect, omnipotent through faith and confidence. No wonder our Lord could say, "Whoever believes in me will perform the same works I do; he will even perform greater works" (cf. John 14:12).

God as Our Spouse in Prayer

When I come to prayer, what joy to know that Christ, that God himself, is my spouse, and that he loves me with the love of benevolence, that is, as his other self. What consolation to know that he takes all my sins away, and fills me with the riches of his infinite goodness. With God I lack nothing, absolutely nothing. Seeing how he has loved me and in a way even more than himself (did he not die that I might live?) am I not drawn to love him more than myself in return? St. Augustine, experiencing this, expressed his longing in the following way, "If I were God, I would want to be Augustine, that God might be God." His joy was so great in being Christ's spouse, that he did not want to see the roles reversed. Here it would almost seem that man has surpassed God in loving, but of course that cannot be. If such a desire is in man it is only an expression of what is first in God. In man it is only a wish, a desire; in God it is something effective. Did not God become man just that we might become God? Who can fathom or understand the heart of God?

As spouses seek unity, so we seek to experience and express our unity with Christ in prayer. If a woman can find such sufficiency in her beloved that she is moved to say, "I just adore him," how much more should we not say this of Christ? Is he not absolutely everything to us? Yes, he is everything to us and he has made it so that we are also everything to him. We need his abundance, but he also needs our emptiness. We complete one another: he by giving, we by receiving. What happiness, what security should be ours in the thought that Christ is everything to us, that we can say with St. Paul, "Who shall separate us from the love of Christ?" (Romans 8:35). Christ is indeed everything to us; he makes up for all that we lack. If we are wanting in love, in humility, in obedience, in self-sacrifice, in prayer, etc., he is there to supply for us. Is not his love, his humility, his obedience, his passion also ours? Nothing can please Jesus more than supplying for everything we lack. This is a fundamental truth of creation and also of redemption. God, in Jesus, wants to be absolutely everything to us, and all he asks is that we receive with faith, with confidence, and with love. Yes, he only asks for absolute faith in his love, a faith and a confidence corresponding to his infinite love and generosity. And then, he wants our love: a love that seeks him as our only good. How then can we ever be discouraged? Our failures, or sins? Why, he wipes them away. Our nothingness and weakness? Why, he fills us with his riches and his power. With him we have absolutely nothing to worry about except to know him, to love him, and to cling to him as our true and only good. All this we should call to mind when at prayer.

Lovers want to exchange confidences and to work together. So it must be with us and Christ. If Christ is really our friend and spouse, we will want to be with him always so as to share our deepest thoughts and feelings. It is here that the Eucharist is so important.

Christ is present everywhere in his divinity, but not in his humanity, which is finite. In his humanity he is certainly present in the sacraments and above all in the Eucharist. There Christ is sensibly present and yet not in a way that destroys the value of our faith. To us beings of sense, this sensible presence has a value we should not ignore. We should love to pray before the tabernacle and we should hunger for daily communion. If we really love Christ as the best of friends, how can we fail to seek to be with him even more than human lovers, who are enamored of each other, seek to be together? We should deeply appreciate communion and the time of thanksgiving after it, when we can, as it were, rest in the arms of Jesus and confide the deepest longings of our hearts to him. The Eucharist is truly our viaticum, Christ walking with us as a friend on the journey through life. Without him, how lonely the journey would be.

Lovers wish to do things for one another. Here we can recall what Christ has done to win each of us as his spouse. It should indeed fill us with joy and gratitude. He saved us not from some temporal death, but from an eternal death, and he did this, not when we were loving and seeking him, but when we had no thought of him, and even when we were offending him. He loves us because he seeks our good, and no sin, no indifference, not even hate on our part can make him cease loving us. If we can show love to someone who saves our life or delivers us from some bondage, should we not love Jesus far more, seeing that he has delivered us from the domination of Satan and the pains of eternal loss? Should not our gratitude, our appreciation, our love be expressed by opening ourselves up unreservedly to his love?

True lovers wish to work together, but the great work of Christ, which he calls us to share, is the salvation of souls. In prayer how can we be unmindful of his interest in this respect? When we see the needs of so many people who do not know him, who do not even seem to care about him, does not our heart suffer with his? If we really love him we cannot but share his joys and sorrows, his victories and setbacks with regard to those he loves: our own brothers and sisters. What an inexhaustible cause for prayer this is.

Of course, in this friendship with Christ our part is more passive. He is all giving and we are all receiving. Hence, we must rest in him through those virtues (sometimes called passive) of faith, confidence, love, obedience, etc. It is by those virtues that we return everything to him enriched with our love. It is here too that the secret of holiness is to be found. Holiness is living the truth, the greatest of which is that God is the Creator, an abyss of all goodness, and we the creature, an abyss of all emptiness. This truth we live through those passive virtues. It is also the secret of pure love. Seeing that God is everything to us, that he loves us because he is good and not because we are, we are moved to love him in return not in order to receive more from him, for he has already given us everything in himself, but just to bear witness to the fact that he is our all. We love him for what he is in himself, and so seek to please him just to bear witness to that fact. Our love becomes pure joy and praise, and our gratitude is without any self-seeking. If we have Christ, what is there that we lack?

As with human lovers, we also want our union with Christ to be permanent. It certainly is on Christ's part, for his will never changes; but we must make it so on our part by never seeking anything apart from him. Our union must in this way be exclusive and in a manner unique, for Christ embraces each and every human person. Hence, in loving him I must love all men as being Christ himself, and they must love me as being Christ himself. Then it is that in Christ we are all made one so that, as St. Augustine says, "There is but one Christ loving himself."

If in spite of all this we still feel miserable and helpless before God in prayer, we can recall that in Christ we share his friendship with his Father. Hence, we can unite with Christ in his total giving of himself to his Father, and know that in Christ we are receiving the total gift of the Father's love in return. In Christ we have perfect access to the Father and share in his life of total giving and receiving in the heart of the Trinity. If we are so loved in Christ, what can be lacking to us? However, if we still find matter for concern because of the uncertainty of the degree of our union with Christ himself, we should remember that this depends wholly on our will, that we need only acknowledge our need of him and accept him as our spouse. But he has also given us something still more here. Christ is our way to friendship with the Father, and Mary is our way to friendship with Christ. She is Christ's perfect spouse even as Christ is the perfect spouse of the Father. Being her children in

Christ, Mary cannot turn us away, and when she brings us to Jesus with herself, he must receive us even as he receives her. Here lies the foundation for St. Louis de Montfort's *True Devotion to the Blessed Virgin.* God has made provision for every contingency; everything is ours just for the asking, just for the willing.

God as Our Life

That God should make us one with himself after the likeness of a bride is indeed something ineffable, and yet even this does not exhaust the full reality of our union with God. Husband and wife do not possess the same organic life. God, however, calls us to share his life even as the branch on the vine and the members of the body share one life; or better, as the body shares in the intellectual life of the soul. This kind of sharing gives a higher and more perfect union, one that God, in his infinite love, has not overlooked.

There is no single comparison which can convey the full reality of this union of man with God. It is a union of two or more persons in one and the same living nature. The only other reality of this kind is the Trinity itself.

113

Indeed Christ uses it as a comparison for our union with himself: "I pray, Father, that they may be one in us, as you are in me and I in you" (cf. John 17:21). This comparison, however, excels the reality of our union with Christ, and although it can enkindle our love, seeing that God offers us something beyond our understanding, still it does not help us much in our understanding of the nature of this union. Hence, we find it more helpful to use several mundane realities and to unite them into one by our imagination. We take the unity of vine and branch, of body and soul, and imagine these parts as being persons united in love after the likeness of bride and bridegroom. Or, we can think of it in this way: if my body were a person distinct from myself, how close would be the love and unity between us?

If we can grasp something of the sharing that goes on between our body and soul, while imagining them both as separate persons, we will get a fair idea of the intimate union that exists between us and Christ by grace. The life of our body, which is material, differs from the life of our soul which is spiritual. So too does our human life differ from God's life, which is divine. Still, in each of these realities both parts are made to work together as one in perfect harmony. In me there is only one responsible agent for both body and soul, because there is only one dominant and responsible director: my will. Whatever I do through my body or through my soul I am the one responsible agent. When a child tells a lie, the mother spanks his body although the lie really came from his mind. Only when my bodily members do something over which my will has no control, does this shared responsibility cease. If my body becomes sick or paralyzed, what results from this is not imputable to me or to my will. We will see that this is likewise true of our union with Christ.

In the union of body and soul we also find that both need each other. Without the body the soul could not express its intellectual activity in the world of matter, and without the soul the body, even if it could have life in itself, would have no intellectual direction; it would be like a brute beast. We seldom think of how intimately our body shares in the activity of our soul. It is by our body that our soul is able to speak, see, hear, write, and make things. It is through our body that we enjoy music, food, and companionship. Every human and rational good is tied up with the body in some way. Of course, the body needs the soul still more. It needs the soul not only in order to live, but also in order to have rational direction. The body does have a direction of its own, but it is only an animal or sensitive direction. If this dominates in man, as in the case of a drunkard, a sex pervert, or a drug addict, the body drags the soul down to its own lower level.

All of this is very applicable to our union with Christ. In him we share in the divine life much as our body shares in our intellectual life except that we are persons. Christ possesses two natures, the human and the divine. In his human nature, he partakes of the divine life through that gift of grace which Adam also had received, but lost by sin. It is only through sharing in this grace, whereby we are made partakers of the divine life, that we become one living reality in Christ after the likeness of an organic unity. Without this life of grace our union with Christ would be no different from that which exists in any human friendship. When, therefore, we accept Christ's offer of friendship through baptism, which is something like a marriage covenant, we are born into this new divine life of grace and become one living organism with Christ. The internal reality of this union is called justification or salvation; its external reality, the visible union of all the faithful, is called the Church, and both together are called the Mystical Body of Christ.

The living principle of this union is the Holy Spirit, God's own Mutual Love, which we receive in Christ. "The Love of God has been poured into our hearts by the Holy Spirit *who* has been given to us" (cf. Romans 5:5). This new life of grace, of which the Holy Spirit himself is the principle, flows into all those who have been baptized into Christ, so that they form one living organism, all united by the bond of Charity, that is, Mutual Love, the Holy Spirit himself. It may be difficult to visualize such a reality, but we have an image of it in our own body. If God can make the trillions of individual cells that make up my body to be me, can he not make all men who are - baptized into Christ, to be Christ's Mystical Body, all of us living by his own divine life of Mutual Love, the Holy Spirit? It is just this which makes that new creature of which St. Paul speaks, "When a man is in Christ, there is a new creature" (cf. Galatians 6:15).

Forming one living being or reality with Christ, we are in a sense one person in him. "You are all one person in Christ" (cf. Gala-

117

tians 3:29). Hence, here too there should be but one dominant and responsible person or director. As the full direction of all his bodily members should be in the power of man's will, so the full direction of all Christ's members should be in the power of Christ's will. When this is so, all that we do is really done by Christ and all that Christ does we do, in and with him. It is only when our wills resist the direction of Christ's Spirit, that our actions are no longer Christ's, but merely our own. Then we are like sick, weak, paralyzed, or even dead members of Christ, no longer responsive to his direction, to his Spirit.

Our goal should be to make our wills so one with Christ through faith and love that we can say with St. Paul, "It is no longer I who live, but Christ who lives in me" (Galatians 2:20). So real is this union, that St. Thomas could say, "The merits and satisfactions of Christ are mine in the same way as though, being in the state of grace, I performed those same works that Christ has done for our salvation" (*Summa* III, 48, 1). That is why our human actions can merit an infinite reward, eternal life; they are the actions of Christ in us. Affectively, that is, in will and desire, this union reaches its climax in the sacrifice of the

Mass. There we are united with Christ in that supreme act of love, whereby, as man, he gives himself to his Father's will, so that his humanity and we in him share in the very act of love whereby as Word he gives himself to his Father in the Trinity. Effectively, this union finds its climax in us when we accept our own death in submission to the Father's will in and with Christ. Then it is that we consummate in Christ his own supreme act of love for his Father, whereby he entered into his glory, so that sharing his sufferings we might also share his glory (cf. Romans 8:17).

As body and soul need each other, so we and Christ also need each other. If Christ is to act in our material world, he needs us, the members of his Mystical Body. In his ordinary providence Christ has chosen to act in this world only through us, his visible members. Hence, Christ still teaches, rules, and ministers to men, but only through certain of his members in the Church, especially through the Pope, bishops, and priests. Even as we seek to manifest our rational life through our body (indeed that is what makes a city differ from a jungle), so Christ seeks to manifest his divine life in the world through us. If all Christ's members were perfectly docile to his

Spirit, Mutual Love, our world would be radiant with true brotherly love and all would know us as the disciples of Christ because of our love for one another. Every Christian would love his brother as Christ himself and be loved by them as being Christ himself. There would be, again, "One Christ loving himself." If Christ needs us, it is still more evident that we need him. Without Christ we would have nothing of the divine life and our goal would be no higher than the human goals of this life. We would be to the divine life somewhat like a madman is to rational life.

Being so one with Christ in this way, our mutual love should be far greater than that which exists between human spouses or which we could imagine would exist between our body and soul were the body a person. Christ, therefore, must love us as himself even as we love our own body; he cannot fail to love us any more than we can fail to love our own body because we are his body. Seeing how Christ loves us, we are drawn to love him in return, for a true lover seeks to love as much as he is loved. But where do I find Christ so as to show him my love? He tells us: "As you did it to one of the least of these my brethren, you did it to me" (Matthew 25:40). Love for our neighbor, therefore, must spring from this desire to make a return of love to Christ. Love of our neighbor is on the other hand the greatest test of our love for God. Hence, "He who says he loves God and hates his brother is a liar" (cf. 1 John 4:20). My brothers are all co-members with me in the Mystical Body of Christ; the gain or loss of one is the gain or loss of all. We form one community in Christ, so that when one suffers we all suffer, and when one rejoices we all rejoice.

We are all one in Christ, but Christ is God; therefore, in him we share in his divine life with his Father even as our body shares in our intellectual human life. As our body could not share more in our intellectual life without itself becoming intellectual, so neither can Christ's humanity, and we in him, share more in the divine life without becoming divine ourselves. In Christ, therefore, all mankind is taken up into the very life of the Trinity. By reason of his humanity, Christ is the one and only bridge whereby we can become partakers of the divine nature and share in the life and friendship of the Trinity. Even as Christ loves us as his other self in human life, so the Father now loves us as his other self in Christ, in his divine life. We have become like unto God himself insofar as that is possible to God's divine power. The Father knows and loves us as his sons in Christ, and we know and love him as our Father in Christ. We share in that total giving and receiving of infinite being that is the very life and joy of the Trinity; we possess eternal life. How true those words of Christ, "I have given the privilege you gave me, that they should all be one as we are one; with me in them and you in me, may they become so perfectly one that the world may know that it was you who sent me and that I have loved them just as much as you have loved me" (cf. John 17:22).

God as Our Life in Prayer

When we come before God in prayer, what a joy to know that at this very moment Christ is loving me as himself, as one of his own members. Hence, he is seeking my good even as he seeks his own good with infinite love. What peace, what confidence this should give. Because he loves me as himself, he shares with me everything he is and has, even as my soul shares all its blessings with my body. Since Christ possesses the totality of all goods, I possess all this in him. Why then should I ever be discouraged? If I do become so, it is because I am looking at myself alone and not at what I am in Jesus.

Christ and I are one and hence whatever Christ does, I do in and with him; and whatever I do through his Spirit, it is he who is acting in me giving my action his infinite value. No wonder St. James in his epistle could say, "The prayer of a just man is powerful before God." Our prayers and our actions have their value from our union with Jesus. Because of this, we can achieve that which lovers so desire, namely, to love even as much as we are loved. No doubt this is because of Christ's gift, but that gift is a reality and with what joy and gratitude it should fill us when we are with him in prayer. So perfect is our union with Christ that we share in him the infinite knowing and loving that is the very life of the Trinity. In Christ we are loved by the Father as being his eternal Son and in Christ we can love and give ourselves to the Father in a perfect return of love. At this very moment we actually possess eternal life: "He who believes in the Son has eternal life" (John 3:36). We have it now, but the full experience of it we will only receive in heaven.

If Christ is everything to us, we are also

everything to him as to his activity in our world. In his love he has deigned to need us, for he wants to give us the opportunity to share his own joy of doing good to others, in saving souls. However, what is most essential here is our perfect submission to his will and guidance even as my body should be perfectly submissive to my will or as a horse should be docile to its rider. Only when we are perfectly submissive to him can he accomplish that which he has planned. If we are not submissive he cannot achieve in this world what he intended to do through us. Here we see how important it is that our prayer should lead us to recognize God's will for us and move us to give ourselves to him in perfect obedience and abandonment. Christ really needs us to help him in the salvation of souls. What a glory, but also what a responsibility.

In wishing to share with us all that he is and has, God has raised us to share in his own life and even in his own activity of saving souls. How wonderful he is in all his works, but especially in effecting man's salvation. All that God does has to be infinitely perfect. If we find it hard to recognize this in his work of salvation (indeed, where do we find absolute perfection among the saved, even among the saints?), this is because we look at salvation as something we achieve rather than as something we receive. Of course, if salvation is something man achieves, it can never be perfect because man himself is so limited; but if it is something God achieves and man receives, then it can be limited only in us and not in itself. Salvation is unique even as a work of God in that it is absolutely perfect not only actively in Christ, but also passively in Mary, who personifies Christ's perfect spouse, the Church, which is "without spot or wrinkle." In other words, not only has Christ done everything that is necessary to unite us in friendship with his Father, but he has also made Mary to be everything that is necessary to unite us in friendship with himself.

Thus, our friendship with God is something we receive only in Christ, and our friendship with Christ is something we receive only in Mary. As there is no access to God except through Christ, so there is no perfect access to Christ except through Mary, through the Church. Salvation is God's most perfect work, and our share in it does not depend on whether we have worked one hour or eleven, but only on that humble confidence which is willing to receive everything with open and loving arms: a love which attests to that greatest of all truths, that the Creator is all giving and the creature all receiving. The extent to which we so open ourselves up to receive everything from God is revealed by our good works and that is their only true value. Our life is to receive everything from God and to return everything to God, the Alpha and Omega. Prayer should give us to see this and move us to live it.

Relation of Knowledge and Affections in Prayer

Having seen what we can know of God through these four comparisons, it would be good to consider a few points on the relationship that exists between knowledge and affections in prayer. Since prayer is a loving converse and an affectionate dealing with God based on the reality of who he is and who we are, it consists essentially in affections, that is, in those desires and choices of the will which motivate our actions. Knowledge simply gives us to know the reality from which such desires and choices should arise. Knowledge in prayer has been compared to the needle which draws through the fabric the golden thread of affections. Once the affections are there, knowledge has finished its task, at least for the moment. Knowledge must go before affections, for we cannot love what we do not know. However, once we love someone, we want to know him still better so as to love him yet more. Thus, knowledge and love have a kind of mutually increasing interaction.

The importance of knowledge, I think, is expressed very well in the statement, "As a man thinks of God, so he stands high or low in the scale of civilization." Knowledge determines our actions; it shows us reality, the true good. Since our last end, which is God, determines all that we do in pursuit of that end, so the quality of our whole life or existence will be reflected by what we think or know of God. If one does not think that God exists, then he makes something else his end, generally himself, to which everything else becomes subjected. If he believes in God, but wrongly considers him as being selfish, he will deal with God as a rival. If he sees him as a cruel master who delights in making him suffer, he will be in open rebellion against God and everything he has made. But, if he sees God as one who loves him more than a maker loves his craft, more than a father loves his child, more than a bridegroom his bride or even more than one loves his own body, then he will be drawn to love God with an equal totality of love. If all men saw God in this way, how different our world would be! It would surely be the kingdom of God on earth.

It has also been said, "If you wish to be loved, love." Nothing draws us to love a person more than his own love for us. Seeing God under the four preceding comparisons helps us to see how much he has loved us. No doubt God could manifest his love in such a way as to overwhelm us, and, as it were, compel us to love him in return. Such a love, however, would not spring so much from within ourselves, from our own goodness of will, as from without. Hence, God reveals himself in little, hidden ways, to whet our appetite and so move us to seek to know him yet more, so as to grow in love. It is here that prayer is essential. Without it we stop at the surface of things, at the sensible, but, "The sensual man understands nothing of the things of God" (cf. Corinthians 2:14).

Holiness or wholeness consists in living according to reality. Now the most basic of all realities, as we have seen, is that God the Creator is all, and that man, the creature, is nothing of himself. Therefore, holiness consists in living this reality before all else. However, because of our pride we are tempted to find our sufficiency in ourselves without God. This is where our four comparisons again help us. They show very clearly how our good lies in God's loving care for us and not in ourselves. What limits God is not his own love, but our willingness to accept his love. It has been aptly said, "It is not our misery that gets in God's way, but our importance." It is with coal that God makes diamonds and from a tiny seed he can bring forth a mighty tree, because these things are entirely subject to his power. God can make us saints without more ado, but only if we fully open ourselves up to him. Did he not do so with the good thief, and with Mary Magdalene?

Knowledge should lead to love and love to action, that is, to the pursuit of the known good. The inner act of love along with other inner acts of the will, such as desire, hope, and fear, are called affections. Affections are the first fruits arising from knowledge, and these should lead to actions by which we pursue the known good. Prayer promotes these inner affections, but the arena in which they are put into practice is our daily life. Prayer, then, stands between knowledge and action. It inspires love, that most powerful of all spiritual forces. Hence, it is the powerhouse which supplies the zest for daily living.

Affections depend on knowledge, of which faith is the greatest source. Hence the importance of faith. Still, faith itself can be considered an affection insofar as it depends on the will. In matters of faith the intellect says, as it were, to the will, "All this is according to reason; it is logical and so has every reason to be true; however, I cannot see the truth itself; it is up to you to accept it or not." The will therefore must command the act of faith; however, it should have logical grounds for doing so; otherwise it is being gullible, like believing that the moon is made of cheese. In the things of faith I cannot understand the truth in itself (for example, how Christ can be God and man); but I have very solid rational grounds for accepting it to be so, especially the historical reality of Christ and his words. Since God is in himself beyond our understanding, almost everything we can know about him in some way depends on faith, on a certain humility of mind that accepts the fact that God is greater than we can understand. Faith gives us to know the reality of the spiritual world, just as our senses give us to know the reality of the material world. When, having the true faith, I step out and act on it, I find that it works. This experience increases my faith, and as I continue to do this, my faith grows and can become as certain to me as sense knowledge.

One of the most important truths of faith, after the existence of God, is that he loves us. It is from this that all other affections flow, for it is because God has first loved us that we are drawn to love him in return. It is here again that our four comparisons are so useful; they help to reveal God's love for us in a very concrete way. By considering God's love for us as revealed in these comparisons, many affections easily arise in our hearts, such as love, adoration, gratitude, joy, confidence, abandonment, obedience, humility, and zeal. By letting our hearts dwell on these affections in prayer or by just resting in the presence of God and letting him impress them on our hearts we find ourselves becoming more and more attached to God as our one and only supreme good. We are then drawn to manifest this as our total choice by our daily actions.

When prayer is filled with consolations, affections come easily and the prayer seems very fruitful. However, there are times when we are dry and sluggish and yet at these times, too, we must make, or rest in, affections if our prayer is to give the desired results or fruits. For such times it is good to have certain fixed affections which we can fall back on. Of these there are four which are most valuable, as we have seen: the four ends of sacrifice, which sum up in a way all our duties toward God. They are: adoration, gratitude, sorrow, and petition. Thus, in prayer we give ourselves to God in adoration as being everything to us as our Creator, Father, Spouse, and Life. Indeed what is there that he is not to us under the likeness of these comparisons? We have received many benefits from God through being our Maker, Father, Spouse, and Life. For all these we offer him our loving gratitude.

When we think of all our failings and lack of love, what a consolation to know that he is ready to forgive us, uniting us again to himself as our Maker, Father, Spouse, and Life. He cannot refuse to forgive us when we ask for pardon, for he is infinitely merciful. We are also very conscious of our many needs and those of others. If we go to God as our Maker, Father, Spouse, and Life, how can he refuse our petitions? When in all this we remember that we are united with Christ in his gift of himself to his Father in adoration, gratitude, reparation, and petition, our prayer has to be most fruitful. Hence, in Christ our prayer is always perfect and most pleasing to God in spite of our feelings to the contrary. This is praying in faith, which is of such great value, because it springs from the inner attachment of the will and not from the immediate satisfaction of the senses.

It is good to remember that affections can be passive as well as active. Indeed, the more passive the better, for then they are more conformed to man's state of dependence on God. As we have seen in these four comparisons, we receive far more from God than we give, for it is only after we have received that we can make a return. Hence, prayer is not just thinking of God or talking to him, it is far more a listening to him. What God has to say to us is far more important than what we have to say to him. Hence, as time goes on, our prayer should become more simple and more passive. We will remain happy just to be in his presence. Actually, the more simple and passive our prayer is, the better — provided there is some awareness of God, which passing distractions do not hinder.

One may ask, "But how does God speak to us?" God speaks to us through actions and events, through his providence. He also speaks to us through inspirations, through the thoughts and desires he puts in our minds or hearts. Of course, since thoughts and desires can come from other sources too, how are we to distinguish? We must judge them by the norms of reason and faith. If they are good they will be conformed to reason and faith and in that case they will be from God in one way or another. If they do not conform to reason and faith then they cannot be good nor therefore from God. When the matter is doubtful we should know that we are free to follow either alternative, although in important matters we should always first seek prudent advice. If God wants us to know or to do something, he can make the matter clear beyond any doubt. If he does not, we should simply judge the matter as best we can and act, knowing that we are doing what God expects of us.

Prayer gives us a living contact with God. This contact is far more important than that we should receive any special vision or feelings in prayer. Also, God has a right to expect us to give a part of our time and attention to him every day. Hence, the most important thing is perseverance in prayer even though we seem to be getting nothing out of it. Prayer is putting ourselves in contact with God and recognizing that he has a right to our time and attention because he is our God. Moreover, we cannot spend time in contact with God without being improved thereby, regardless of feelings to the contrary.

Variety of Ways

Our end is to know reality: who God is and who we are, and then to live this out in our daily lives. This knowledge God offers to each person in different ways according to his own particular needs and circumstances. Every person is a priceless gem to God, and so in his loving providence he is arranging everything to bring out the fullest possible beauty of that gem. God has placed men in every walk of life and given them a great variety of natural gifts, temperaments, and talents, because he wants to show that sanctity is possible to everyone and even at any moment in life. God can raise up saints from the dung heap, so to speak, and in a moment.

The variety of means whereby God leads people applies also to prayer. Here too his gifts are manifold so that there are many different forms of prayer and in these forms many degrees or steps. God may lead one through many forms of prayer or he may keep him in much the same form all his life. Thus some may find vocal prayer as their habitual or special way to God, others some form of meditative prayer.

What we must especially keep in mind is that God is free to lead each person as he sees best and by any form of prayer he chooses, and that sanctity is possible to everyone. All that is required is docility to God's guiding action. Hence, we should pray as God gives us to pray and not strive for some kind of prayer, which although better in itself, may not be what God wants of us. One can always go to God as a living and real person, as a friend who loves him more than anyone else in the world. How he does this will depend on his own personality and God's grace, but the fact that he does it is the main thing, and that is coming to God by prayer.

Since God is our Creator and we his creatures, it belongs to his infinite wisdom and love to arrange all the circumstances of our lives. Our part is to believe in his loving care and to accept whatever he sends us as the best means for obtaining our goal which is himself, our eternal Beatitude. God is everything to us after the likeness of a Maker, Father, Spouse, and Life, but it is only through living with God a life of love in the light of these comparisons that we come to experience their full reality. This cannot be done without prayer. Prayer alone introduces us into the promised land where God dwells and there gives us, through faith, to share his own beatitude, the mutual knowing and loving that is the very life of God himself in his Trinity of persons.

How true those words of St. Paul, "Such is the richness of the grace which he has showered on us. He has let us know the mystery of his purpose, that he would bring everything together under Christ as head, everything in the heavens and everything on earth. And it is in him that we are claimed as God's own" (cf. Ephesians 1:7-11).

CHAPTER 3

"Why Have You Forsaken Me?"

The Contemplative Life

There is a growing interest in contemplation today, arising partly from Vatican II but also from a contact with Eastern religions. Today's youth are seeking experience as a criterion of reality. Institutional religions appear to be formal and dead, producing no results. Also, the utopia of science and material progress has proven itself illusory. Theories and dogmas are looked down on, so that many are turning to Eastern religions which seem to offer results through definite methods and practical techniques. In the midst of all this, Christians are reminded that there is a way of experiencing God in their own tradition.

Experience has its value, but dangers too. Whatever is real should produce results; look at what the sun effects. Now if God exists he should produce even greater results. Yet the problem may not be with results, but with our recognizing them. God is effecting far more than the sun, but we are so involved in secondary causes we do not recognize him, the first cause. On the other hand, experience is no necessary criterion of reality. A trip on LSD can be real, but the resulting experiences are not. One may dream that he is a king; the dream is a reality, but not that he is a king. Again one may feel that God has rejected him because of some sin; the feeling is real, but contrary to the truth of God's mercy and forgiveness.

Experience is generally related to the senses and has value, but reality as known by reason and faith is far greater. Reason and faith must be our main guides to truth. If we act according to these we will soon come to experience their reality. In the Gospel Christ always asked for faith. If we have faith the rest will follow.

In this chapter I am mainly concerned

with the experience of God found in Christian contemplation. After defining contemplation and presenting its main divisions, a section is devoted to the Christian life since contemplation is ordered to lead us to this as its end. However, my main concern will be to show how one develops in a life of prayer through the two purgative nights, of which St. John of the Cross speaks, and how these end in one of two kinds of contemplation: spiritual or mystical.

What Is Contemplation?

A short but adequate definition of contemplation is, "It is a simple intuition of the truth." The term intuition shows that it is a receiving rather than an active seeking. When we contemplate, for example, a sunset, we do not go out and try to get it; we simply let its beauty enter into us: that is the meaning of contemplation. When we say it is the intuition of the "truth," we indicate the object of contemplation which is something considered primarily as true.

Because truth can come to us in different ways, contemplation can be divided into natural and supernatural, according as the source of this truth is either natural or supernatural. Since natural truth can be received either through the senses or through the intellect, natural contemplation itself is of two kinds: sensible (such as the contemplation of a mountain, the sea, or a sunset), or intellectual. A good example of this latter is that enlightenment to which most Eastern forms of contemplation aspire, such as Zen or Yoga. Our intellect has a capacity for pure intelligible truth without sensible images somewhat as is proper to the angels. St. Thomas (*Summa* I, 94, 1) says that we are impeded at present from such knowledge of intelligible truth through being distracted and preoccupied with sensible things. Therefore, by withdrawing our minds from such sensible images, we can apparently come in time to experience a certain intuition of intelligible truth, that is, of pure being, which is called enlightenment.

If the truth we are contemplating is supernatural, that is, known by divine revelation, then contemplation is again divided into two kinds: mystical and spiritual. Mystical, also called infused contemplation, is a free gift from God which cannot be merited, but for which one can only dispose himself. This kind of contemplation is recognized by all and so its existence presents no difficulty. Spiritual contemplation is a term I prefer to use to designate that contemplation which has generally been called active or acquired contemplation or even simply prayer, such as the prayer of simplicity, naked faith, and simple regard. These terms are all misleading and do not convey the true nature of this contemplation, which is just as truly such as is mystical contemplation. Mystical contemplation is indeed also spiritual, but still, because it is something more, reserving the term spiritual, for this other kind of contemplation adequately distinguishes the two. The other terms mentioned above are inadequate because this contemplation is not active but passive, nor is it acquired, for it too is a gift of God's grace, but within the ordinary realm of grace. Neither can this contemplation be rightly called some simple form of prayer, for it is intuitive and passive, characteristics proper to contemplation. For all these reasons I have chosen to call this contemplation spiritual, and I see it as another form of supernatural contemplation in many ways equal to mystical contemplation.

Contemplation is the intuition of the

truth, and supernatural contemplation the intuition of that truth which concerns our relationship with God by reason of his revealed plan. In order to understand supernatural contemplation and how it functions, we must first know something of God's plan for us, how it is to be achieved, and in what its final perfection consists.

God's Plan in Creating

When God created, he had a reason, and this reason had to be love for himself, since nothing else existed. It also had to be in order to give, since, being infinitely perfect, he could not act in order to receive anything. These two conditions were fulfilled by God creating, out of love for his own goodness and happiness, in order to share these with others. God's happiness consists in friendship, in that mutual knowing and loving and being known and loved that goes on between the three divine persons in the Trinity. That we might share in this, God had to make us free, for friendship cannot be forced. But this very freedom exposes us to the danger of pride, to a false idea of ourselves in our relationship with God. Hence, we are tempted to seek our well-being in ourselves independent of God. Lucifer fell into this error and so did Adam, and from the effects of his fall we are all suffering. Because of this we all begin life with a false idea of ourselves and of our relationship with God. Certainly the most basic of all truths is that God, the Creator, is all and we, the creatures, are nothing. If contemplation is the intuition of the truth it is this truth above all that we must see and live.

The importance of realizing this can be shown by a couple of examples. If a child has a false idea of himself in his relationship with his parents, he may think that he must earn his own living and make his own way in life. Imagine all the worries, fears, and anxieties a little child would have laboring under such a false idea. However, once he comes to recognize his true relationship with his parents, how different things become. He then sees how they wish to care for all his needs and so his worries vanish and he enjoys that wonderful freedom which is the privilege of children. Another example is that of a king who chooses to marry a poor beggar-girl. If she has a false idea of what he expects of her, she may either feel that she must give or do something great for him or that she should shy away from him through a sense of total unworthiness. However, what he actually expects is that she simply receive all that he wishes to give her and then give it all back to him enriched with her personal love. It is such a view of our relationship with God that contemplation should give us.

Three Lives in Us

In order to understand the process by which we come to contemplation and live the above truth, we must know that there are three lives in us: our bodily life which is animal, our intellectual life which is rational, and the divine life of God which we have by grace. When several lives are united and ordered to work together in unison, the lower life must always be subject to the direction of the higher; otherwise the higher life is degraded. A good example of this is the unity that should exist between a horse and its rider. A horse running away with its rider is certainly not an ideal situation. Rather the good of both horse and rider requires that the horse be so perfectly submissive to the guidance of its rider that it is given to share in man's higher life and goals. But for this it must be broken in; it must be made to renounce its own way of knowing and acting so as to be perfectly submissive to man's higher knowledge and direction. In other words it must lose its own lower life so as to share in the higher life of man.

If man is to share in God's higher life and happiness, his lower bodily life and rational life must be brought into subjection to God's Life and Spirit in much the way way. If man allows his bodily life to dominate him he becomes like an animal, and the fruits of such a life are those of corrupt nature which St. Paul enumerates (see Galatians 5:19): feuds, drunkenness, orgies, etc. If man brings his bodily life into subjection to reason, then his body is given to share in his intellectual activity, as is evident in every craft. Moreover, if through faith man's reason is brought into perfect subjection to the Spirit of God living within him, then the reign of God's life of divine charity will become manifest among men and Christ's prayer will be fulfilled: "That they may be one even as we are one."

From this it is evident that the spiritual life consists in a twofold submission or purgation which St. John of the Cross calls nights, wherein man's bodily or sensual life is brought into subjection to his reason and rea-

147

son in its turn is subjected to God. Of course, it is the higher life that subjects the lower to itself. It is man who breaks in the horse, not the horse that breaks in itself. This is likewise true with regard to ourselves and God. It is our reason that must make our body subject to itself, and God who must subject both our reason, and through it our body, to himself by faith. However, there are some differences here. Being intellectual, we are free and so we can know and cooperate with God, or choose not to. Hence, in this work of purgation there is an active part, that which we can do, and a passive part, that which God does in us. Also, although we divide this work of purgation into two stages or nights, namely, one of the senses and the other of the spirit, still both parts are purged together and it is only a matter of which is being predominately purged.

Hence, in this work of purgation we find that the active part is never wholly separated from the passive part. Also, while the senses are being brought into subjection to reason through faith, in the night of the senses, reason itself is also being subjected to faith in some degree, and it is only when reason is fully subjected to faith, in the night of the spirit, that the senses themselves become perfectly subject, since they depend on reason. Thus, man and God both work together in the growth of the divine life in man.

Perfection of the Christian Life

Now that we understand God's plan for us and how it is achieved, let us look at its final goal. This, St. John of the Cross tells us, is union with God, which can be of two kinds: substantial, that which all creatures have with God by nature, since God is giving them existence, or by likeness, that by which a soul through grace is transformed into God by a union of wills, that is, by friendship. This is perfectly achieved when our will becomes one with God's so that there is no longer any disparity between his will and ours.

Such a union can only be effected through faith, for faith alone can give us to know God and his will as they truly are so as to unite ourselves with him in charity. Faith, therefore, must be our only guide so that whenever the desires of our senses or the views of our reason are contrary to the dictates of faith, we always renounce these and act according to faith in love. Perfection consists in bringing our senses and our reason into perfect submission to God's will as known through faith. Then we no longer live our own life, but Christ and his Spirit live in us. Thus, we become so perfectly docile to God's will, that, in a way, God and we have but one life and one activity, and God lives as perfectly within us as he does within himself. That is perfection.

In the Gospel our Lord never asked us to become enlightened nor that we should become mystics. He only asked that we believe, that we have faith, and the hope and love that flow from faith.

Hence, St. John of the Cross in his *Ascent of Mount Carmel* makes the very important statement that the road to union with God and so to perfection consists not in multiplying ways and methods of prayer nor in any consolation, necessary though these be for beginners, but in just one thing, namely, in the ability to deny oneself truly for Christ's sake of all things from within and from without, and indeed, the soul which does this will find therein all these other experiences and more, while the soul which does not will get no place (cf. Bk. 2, Ch. 7). By the ability to deny oneself, he does not mean doing many penances, but that we are ready to renounce the desires of our senses and the judgments of our reason whenever these are not in perfect conformity with God's will as known by faith.

The Two Nights in General

The end of the Christian life is to become so perfectly docile to the action of the Holy Spirit that we no longer use our bodily or intellectual faculties according to their own impulses, but only as directed by the Holy Spirit through faith. This goal is effected according to St. John of the Cross by a twofold purgation which he calls the night of the senses and the night of the spirit. Both of these nights have an active part, that which we can do, and a passive part, that which God does in us.

Since contemplation is essentially something passive, a taking in, an allowing something to be done to us, supernatural contemplation starts with the first passive night, that is, the night of the senses. This is clearly the teaching of St. John of the Cross, for it is at this moment that the Holy Spirit begins to take over and reduces the activity of the soul. It becomes a moment of crisis since one finds it difficult to understand what is happening. God seems to be out to destroy everything we thought was good and to be preserved. Hence, one is in need of a good director who understands this action of God; otherwise much harm may result either by straining for something God no longer expects or by giving up the pursuit of holiness as something impossible. St. John of the Cross is very hard on ignorant confessors who misguide souls at this point in the spiritual life.

In one who is seriously giving himself to a life of prayer, the night of the senses generally starts quite early. Religious may readily begin to experience it during the time of their temporary vows. Really there can be no solid life of faith without it, since its very purpose is to raise one above the things of sense to the realities of faith. Therefore, since all Christians are called to live a life of faith, contemplation need not and should not be something rare in the Christian life. However, since it is quite evident that very few have mystical contemplation, there must be some other form of contemplation that is just as truly from God, but which is not mystical. It is this that I call spiritual contemplation.

One may ask why St. John of the Cross never refers to this other kind of contemplation. My answer is that although he does not refer to it directly, neither does he exclude it.

In fact both he and St. Teresa acknowledge that God has his exceptions and that he can and does lead some to perfection without mystical contemplation. There are good reasons to hold that this spiritual contemplation which was an exception in their day is more the rule in our day. We know that mysticism has flourished at certain times and places. We may not know all the reasons for this, but certainly the social and spiritual conditions of the time had something to do with it. We can also know that it certainly was not because people were more generous then than now. When one reads of the many aberrations which St. John and St. Teresa ran into among their own religious and the laity in their day with regard to mysticism, one realizes that souls were just as subject to pride, vanity, and self-seeking then as now.

If mystical prayer is a free gift which cannot be merited, and if contemplation is necessary for Christian perfection and even, in a rudimentary form, for salvation, then there must be another kind of contemplation that is possible through ordinary grace and available to all.

Much of the confusion that has arisen concerning contemplation comes from the failure to recognize this fact. Hence, we can see the difficulty experienced when some tried to hold that mystical contemplation rather than contemplation of some kind is in the ordinary way of the spiritual life. Mystical and spiritual contemplation are two forms of supernatural contemplation both of which are capable of leading one to Christian perfection. Apparently God calls some to one and some to the other according as he sees which is best for their sanctification. Let us now see how the two nights work in leading the soul into contemplation and so to Christian perfection.

Active Night of the Senses

St. John of the Cross says that the passive night of the senses comes not at the beginning of the spiritual life, but only after one has come to know God to some degree through the lights and consolations of prayer and has become united to him in a love that is now strong enough to endure some difficulty in his service. This moment will come sooner to recollected souls, those who are more earnest in their search for God. This is where the active night can help. We can prepare ourselves for the passive night by withdrawing our senses from creatures and centering them on God alone in prayer.

Apparently this can be done in two ways. One is that which is more traditional in the West, namely, through meditative prayer and Christian mortification. St. John of the Cross and St. Teresa seem to have considered only this way. The other way is that which has been more traditional in the East, but also found in the West, namely, of withdrawing the mind from the consideration of all sensible reality to center it either on being as intelligible in itself, as does Zen and Yoga, or on some simple word or concept of God, as recommended in the *Cloud of the Unknowing.* All of these can be called forms of active contemplation and no more. This withdrawal method has one advantage in that it pacifies one's faculties and so dispose him for passive contemplation, but it also has one disadvantage in that the mind is not therein necessarily enlightened by faith. Hence, for a Christian this must be supplied by some kind of reflective reading on the truths of faith as found in Scripture.

The active night of the senses consists in doing what we can to withdraw ourselves from sensible creatures so as to seek our good and happiness in God alone. In this regard St.

John of the Cross points out the harm that can come from seeking our end in sensible creatures. Not only do they deprive us of God as being false ends, but they also weary, torment, blind, defile, and weaken the soul for they cannot give, but rather hinder, us from our true good which by nature we really desire. He also gives several lists of counsels, such as always seeking that which is more painful, dissatisfying, and laborious, rather than that which is more pleasant, satisfying, and easy. These must be rightly understood; otherwise, they could put one in a spiritual bind. We should act in this way only when all other things are equal, that is, when we have no good reason for choosing what is less painful, etc. One then chooses the more difficult only because he seeks to acquire a mastery over his sense-desires.

This active night will be practiced somewhat differently by those who give themselves to Eastern forms of prayer. These withdraw themselves from sensible things through the very form of their prayer. Sensible things are of no value to them compared to the higher knowledge of the spirit which they seek. However, after their prayer they must live out this evaluation in their daily life and in this they do not differ from what St. John of the Cross recommends.

Since what we can do in this night of withdrawing ourselves from sensible things is very little because of our superficial understanding of what is fully required, God must take over the work in the passive night of the senses. When he does so he seems to be out to destroy everything we thought was good and valuable. This proves how wholly inadequate we ourselves are to accomplish this work of purgation.

Passive Night of the Senses

In the passive night God begins to take over the direction of the soul's purgation and sanctification. This is necessary because beginners in the spiritual life mix up much self-seeking with their pursuit of God, especially by their attachment to sensible consolations. Then, too, they give too much importance to their own activity as though they were the chief agent of their sanctification and God merely their helper. Hence, they are inclined to seek spiritual things in a natural and selfish way and this gives rise to many imperfections connected with the seven capital sins, such as pride, avarice, gluttony, and envy. In the passive night God is out to cure all these defects by bringing us to a true knowledge of ourselves in relation with him.

St. John of the Cross gives three signs by which one can know when this night begins. Although he applies them to those who are seeking God by the way of meditation, they also apply to those who are practicing some Eastern form of active contemplation, except for the first sign which is that one finds he can no longer meditate as before without great effort or strain. This inability to meditate is now experienced as something more habitual. One is drawn to be more quiet, but fears that in doing so he will be wasting his time.

The second sign is that one finds pleasure neither in the things of God, which now leave him dry, nor in the things of sense, which he does not esteem or desire. This does not mean that one cannot find satisfaction in the things of sense; indeed, there is a real temptation to go back to them, but one does not want to, for he knows that they cannot really satisfy him.

The third sign is that one finds in himself a general longing for God together with a fear that he is falling away from him through his own fault. This is the best sign for it proves that this state is of God and not due to the soul's own negligence, for then there would not be this fear of falling away. Along with spiritual dryness one also experiences a great spiritual weakness, so much so that he finds strength neither to keep resolutions nor even to make them. This night generally is accompanied by other trials too, such as sickness, misunderstandings, scruples, and a sense of aimlessness. Strong temptations against faith, patience, or purity may also assail the soul. All this is aimed at leading us to the truth of who God is and who we are.

All souls must go through some form of this passive night if they are to come to supernatural contemplation. A self-achieved supernatural contemplation is as much of a contradiction as a self-achieved supernatural salvation. However, this night need not come exactly as St. John of the Cross and others explain it. They are speaking of souls who are sincerely seeking God through a life of prayer. Even these experience it in different ways and in different degrees of intensity according to God's plan and their own generosity. For some it lasts for years; others may experience it through one or more severe trials, while still others may receive it in small parcels over a long period of time. Also, since God seeks the salvation and sanctification of all men, he has other ways of tearing those not given to prayer from sensible creatures and leading them to live for the higher goods of faith. This he may do through marital or financial problems, through some humiliating sickness or even through the weakness of old age which destroys the dreams of youth and makes one realize his need for the higher realities of faith.

During this night one feels very confused and lost, but near the end God generally begins to give him some little insight into what he has been doing. When the full revelation does come, he experiences a great peace and joy not unlike that which a small lost child would experience on finding its loving parents. One comes to know his true self, that is, himself in his true relationship with God, which is like to that of a child with its parents. He then understands why he who humbles himself as a little child is the greatest in the kingdom of heaven. One no longer seeks his joy and security in himself, but only in God. His feelings find their best expression in the words of Our Lady's Magnificat, "He who is mighty has done great things in me and holy is his name." Since it was the very experience of his misery that has given him to see his true relationship with God, he cries out with St. Paul, "Willingly will I glory in my infirmities that the power of Christ may dwell in me."

There are three basic fruits which flow from this passive night; all are fruits of contemplation, that is, of seeing the truth of who God is and who we are. They are proper to this night regardless of how one may have experienced it. The first is a joyful humility; this comes from seeing who we are in relation to God. There is perhaps no greater joy in the spiritual life than to experience one's nothingness while at the same time experiencing God's all-powerful and loving care. The second fruit is confidence, which comes from seeing who God is, especially in seeing that he loves us not because we are good, but because he is good. Both of these, humility and confidence, give rise to a distrust of self so that we no longer look for success from our own activity, but only from perfect docility to God's leading action. The third fruit is a great growth in faith, and therefore also, in hope and charity which depend on faith. During this night one has only faith in God's love to go on, for everything else is taken away. Experiencing how richly his faith has been rewarded, he is greatly strengthened to hold on to faith in all future trials. This night is indeed a "happy chance" when one goes forth from himself to find his beloved in a way he never dreamed. Having now found his true relationship with God, all those faults connected with the seven capital sins seem to vanish of themselves. The blessings of perseverance through this night are indeed many and great.

Period Between the Nights of Sense and Spirit

On coming out of the night of the senses one experiences a period of spiritual peace and joy; he is like one freed from prison, or like one coming into the light from a dark cave. While contemplation starts with the night of the senses, it comes to a certain flowering when one emerges from it. This flowering is of two kinds, mystical and spiritual, and these two are different.

St. John of the Cross sees mystical contemplation as the normal outcome of the night of the senses. Indeed, there is no better way of experiencing the great contrast that exists between our own nothingness (which this night has impressed upon us) and God's all-powerful goodness than the gift of infused contemplation. This gift is the most certain sign of emergence from the night of the senses and is the beginning of a period of great joy and consolation. However, this new period is still punctuated with trials and weaknesses, thus showing that the work of purgation is not yet wholly completed.

Those who emerge from the night of the senses with spiritual contemplation do so by receiving a very clear light of what God has done and taught them and also of all the blessings he has given them through the darkness and sufferings of this night. Seeing how wonderfully God supplies for our human weakness and nothingness, one finds great joy in the newly discovered relationship he now sees he has with God. Seeing also how God has effected all these blessings through such darkness and weakness, he is ready to continue on in this same way, and even tells God so. Actually he does continue on in much the same way, but now with a somewhat different point of view. Having once seen the fruit of such trials, subsequent sufferings are not so distressing, for he knows that they will have a fruitful outcome even though he cannot clearly see what this will be in each case. Thus, one continues to grow through alternating periods of trials and lights; the trials usually preparing the way for the subsequent light. One must live wholly by faith, but the contents of this faith become ever more manifest as each trial ends with new insights.

This period of peace and consolation will last for a longer or shorter time, but end it must, for greater purgation is still required. Of those who have received mystical contemplation only a few go on to experience the night of the spirit in the drastic way explained by St. John of the Cross. The greater number will be purified by alternating trials and mystical consolations, the trials being the more predominant. Those who receive spiritual contemplation are purified in much the same manner, but their trials alternate with spiritual lights rather than with mystical experiences.

Active Night of the Spirit

The purpose of the night of the spirit is to bring our spiritual or rational faculties into perfect submission to God's higher life so that we use these faculties, as well as our senses, only as directed by God through faith. This is partly accomplished in the night of the senses, but it must now be achieved more completely.

When we speak of the active night of the spirit we are speaking about the practice of mortifying our spiritual faculties which should accompany the mortification of the senses in the active night of the senses, but should also carry on into the passive nights as offering what we can do to cooperate with God's action therein. Although it is necessary even for salvation to bring our spiritual faculties of intellect, memory, and will into submission to faith in some basic way, we are concerned here with that more perfect submission which is required for perfect union of the soul with God.

St. John of the Cross tells us that the intellect can have two sources of knowledge, one natural and the other supernatural. Natural knowledge is received from the senses, both exterior and interior, and from the intellect's own reasoning activity. On the other hand supernatural knowledge is received through some form of higher enlightenment from God. This may be of corporeal things, received either through the exterior senses, such as visions and locutions, or through the interior senses, such as meditation and reflection. It may be of spiritual things, received either in a clear and distinct way, through spiritual visions and locutions or through revelations and spiritual feelings, or it may be received in a general and obscure way, such as comes through faith.

St. John of the Cross tells us that we must simply ignore the knowledge that comes to us from any of these sources except from faith. Only insofar as all such knowledge can serve faith does it have any value, even as the animal knowledge of a horse has no human value except insofar as it can serve the directions it receives from its rider.

Hence, he counsels us, we must give no value to any mystical experience beyond the immediate effect which they produce in us but without us. We should not even worry whether these impressions come from God or from the devil, but simply go on serving God as known through faith alone. Only with regard to the higher mystical graces of substantial touch and substantial words does St. John of the Cross allow a different approach: these are part of our union with God and so we may be humbly resigned in their regard, neither desiring or not desiring them.

As for the memory it merely recalls what the intellect has previously known. Hence, we should place no value or hope whatsoever in recalling any of the above knowledge except insofar as it will help us to live more perfectly by faith.

The will is our most important faculty, for all the strength of our soul is contained in its faculties with their passions, all of which are subject to the will. Hence, if the will controls and directs all of these to God alone as known by faith, then all the strength of the soul is kept for God. This is achieved when, as St. John of the Cross tells us, we so control our four basic passions of joy, hope, fear, and grief that these never react to any good or evil except as revealed by faith. Hence, our evaluation of any good, whether temporal (riches, rank, etc.), natural (health, beauty, wisdom, etc.), sensual (pleasure through the senses), moral (virtues and observance of the law), supernatural (miracles and other gifts), or spiritual (prayer, penances, Church, sacraments, etc.) — our evaluation must be made according to faith and nothing else.

Thus, all the powers of the soul are kept for God alone, that is, subject to his guidance coming to us through faith.

If we could so bring all our faculties into perfect submission to God's guidance as known through faith, we could come to perfect union with God through our own efforts. But this is impossible for a number of reasons, and hence the necessity of the passive night of the spirit. First of all, it is one thing to know something in theory and quite another to put it into practice. Nothing is easier than humility in theory, but nothing more difficult in practice, that is, to come to a deep conviction of our nothingness. This is because we are so inclined to rest on our own human way of knowing and desiring that we are often unable to see when these are not in agreement with faith. Hence, there remain in us the roots of habits and affections for creatures which even the night of the senses was not able to fully eradicate. Our spirit also clings to external things and is distracted and influenced by them far more than we can perceive. Then, too, we have an imperfect concept of our true relationship with God and this results in a very imperfect faith, confidence, abandonment, docility, and the like. Those who have been enjoying mystical prayer are also in danger of giving these experiences a value which draws them away from the purity of faith and love which they should have. For all these reasons the passive night of the spirit is necessary if the soul is to come to any degree of perfect union with God.

In the passive night of the spirit man's spiritual faculties are now purged or brought into more complete submission to God's divine life through the direction and powerful action of God's divine attributes. Although these may work differently in those called to mystical contemplation than in those called to spiritual contemplation, the end to be achieved is the same for both. In mystical contemplation the divine attributes assail the soul with powerful but painful mystical experiences proportionate to former consolations. In spiritual contemplation these attributes work in a more ordinary and hidden way through various trials and lights. The soul is passive as to these alternating experiences, but it is able to cooperate with them by using its faculties in a normal way.

In this passive night one is given to experience in such a deep and penetrating way what faith tells us about who God is and who we are that one is led into a living conformity with this reality. This is effected through the divine attributes. God's truth so assails the soul with divine light that our own light seems to be utter darkness. His sanctity so exposes our inner discord and sinfulness that holiness seems utterly impossible to us. His omnipotence overwhelms us with our own nothingness and lack of all power. His infinite goodness makes us see our own total emptiness and lack of all good. God's wisdom confronts us with our blindness and inability to guide and direct ourselves. It is through such experiences, like fire clearing away all opposing moisture in wood, that we are brought to a living experience of faith and so made capable of being united with God in the consuming fire of divine love. This passive night is aimed at bringing us into a full experience of the truth of who God is and who we are, so that we see ourselves as a little child who finds its total well-being in the loving care of its parents. Faith tells us all this, but it is only the actual experience of it that can convince us and move us to act consistently in conformity with it.

During this night both the mystic and the spiritual contemplative will act in much the same way, even though their experiences are different. The mystic will act differently only when he is enjoying infused prayer wherein he is more passive. Otherwise, both must act in much the same way and first of all by placing no value on any source of knowledge other than faith, making it alone the foundation of their hope and love. They must also be faithful to definite times of prayer, regardless of how useless this may seem to be. They must strive to be perfectly submissive to every indication of the divine will in a spirit of perfect abandonment and obedience. Their trust in God must never fail, no matter what he sends them, even if they must cry out with Job, "Even if he kills me, yet will I trust him." They must be willing to go on in darkness, not knowing where God is leading them, but certain that he is doing so. As they progress they will find that they must put less and less value on their own activity and more in being attentive to God's leading action alone. In general they must learn to wait in patience for the Lord with nothing more than a deep yearning for him. Mystical and spiritual contemplatives must indeed act in much the same way, and yet God acts quite differently in them.

When we come to consider the fruits of this night, we find that they are not much different from those of the previous night of the senses, but only deeper and more intense. They all spring from experiencing more deeply and fully, through the action of God's divine attributes, what faith tells us of who God is and who we are. The peace, then, which this night gives is far greater than that of the former night. Its blessings may be summed up as follows: first, it gives a spirit of salvation, for seeing that our good lies only in God's infinite and immutable love for us, and not in ourselves, we experience a great sense of security and salvation. We also experience a joyful humility and an unshakable confidence. This comes from seeing that our weakness is the very reason why God takes such wonderful and loving care of us. A strong estimative love is also a fruit of this night. We come to see so clearly how God is our only true good that we can no longer deliberately seek our good elsewhere. We also experience an ever-growing docility to the Holy Spirit and attentiveness to his action.

Admiring how God turns every event and even every suffering to our good, we want to be ever more conscious of and submissive to his action. Our life becomes more simple and unified as we see how God has made us one with himself and with all other creatures in

Christ. We find too a pure joy in creatures for, no longer seeking them as ends, we find in them a beautiful though partial revelation of God himself. Finally, our love becomes pure; seeing how we have everything in God's love for us and that he loves us because he is good and not because we are good, we now love him not to receive anything from him, for we have everything already in his love for us, but only to testify to him that he is our all and our only true good.

These blessings are all experienced by both mystical and spiritual contemplatives, but somewhat differently. The mystic experiences them in a more intuitive way, and in him they find their peak in mystical marriage. The spiritual contemplative experiences them in a normal and more reasoned way and in him they find their peak in a certain unified vision of all things in God through the humanity of Christ or his Mystical Body or in some other basic supernatural truth. Mystics tend to manifest these blessings by intuitive insights and sayings which are very moving, whereas spiritual contemplatives manifest them more by clear reasonings that carry great inner conviction. These blessings do not come suddenly nor are they static; but they come gradually, especially in spiritual contemplatives, and keep growing even unto death.

The Two Ways

It should now be clear that God has two ways of leading souls through contemplation to perfection. Since the very essence of union with God consists in bringing ourselves, that is, our faculties, into submission to the higher life and action of God, which also requires a certain passivity on our part, we can say that contemplation in some rudimentary form is even necessary for salvation. Hence, there is something of contemplation in the very essence of the Christian life. Certainly some degree of prayer is necessary, for one cannot be aware even of God's existence if he is so taken up with the things of sense and reason that he never even thinks of God. However, such prayer, if it is to conform to the truth, must be contemplative, that is, passive to some degree, for it must show that our salvation consists in receiving from God's bounty and not in our own self-achievement.

Contemplation in some degree is necessary for salvation, but if all souls are not given mystical contemplation, then there must be another kind of supernatural contemplation by which all men can come to God, namely, spiritual contemplation. Why God gives mystical contemplation to some and not to others, is God's own secret. Certainly it is not because some souls are more generous or faithful than others. There are many religious who can say with the Little Flower that they have not deliberately refused God anything (if not from the age of three at least from the time they have given themselves to God in religion). We are inclined to judge generosity by success which is very misleading, as the following will show. If I have a fault and I make a real effort and succeed in correcting it, I feel that I have been generous; if I have the same fault, make the same effort, but fail, I feel wanting in generosity. However, if I accept this humiliation I will be greater before God. The only criterion, therefore, of one's generosity is that he does not knowingly or deliberately do anything contrary to God's will; that alone is within the power of our free will.

If mystical contemplation were a sign of a higher form of holiness, then all mystics should be holier than all nonmystics, which is certainly not true. We find some mystics who were great saints and others who were not; but we also find some spiritual contemplatives who were great saints and others who were not. St. Thomas Aquinas was a great saint and also a great contemplative; however, it was only near the end of his life that he received that mystical grace after which he was no longer able to continue his work on the *Summa Theologica*. Who would say that he became a saint only with or after this mystical grace? If he had been a mystic before, at least to this extent, we would never have had his great theological works which have all the signs of being the fruit of spiritual contemplation.

Another reason why some look upon mystical contemplation as something superior in the spiritual life is because the gifts of the Holy Spirit are very operative therein. No doubt these gifts are more manifest in the mystic, but that does not mean that they are less operative in spiritual contemplatives. Actually St. Thomas says that the gifts of the Holy Spirit are necessary for salvation (*Summa* III, 68, 2). Hence, they must be operative in every Christian to some extent. They are indeed very operative in the spiritual contemplative, but in a more subtle and ordinary way.

Although we may not know all the reasons why God calls some souls to mystical contemplation and others to spiritual contemplation, we cannot doubt that these are two authentic forms of supernatural contemplation. Both are prayer and both are passive, but to different degrees. Both are based on faith and can lead to the perfection of charity, that is, to a perfect union of the will with God's will. God seeks the salvation and sanctification of all men. If, therefore, he calls some to mystical contemplation and others to spiritual contemplation, it must be because he knows they will be better sanctified by one than by the other. It may also be because one way will better equip one for the special work God wishes him to accomplish. This seems quite evident in the life of St. Thomas Aquinas.

Which Is More Sanctifying?

Seeing that these are two ways in which God leads us to him, we are naturally inclined to ask which is the more sanctifying. Of course, we cannot give any real answer to this, for we have no absolute way of judging the degree of one's charity or holiness. There are, however, some external signs (such as the practice of the virtues); but since even these are influenced very much by one's natural dispositions we have no fully adequate means for making such a judgment. Still, there are a few points worthy of consideration which will help us to see that one way may be just as sanctifying as the other.

We are naturally inclined to think that mystical contemplation is more sanctifying because God's action appears to be more powerful therein, but this can be misleading. Dom John Chapman, speaking of enclosed orders, says in his *Spiritual Letters* (p. 113), "Some of the most saintly are not mystics at all. It seems to me that people can get to very extraordinary sanctity and a wonderful love of God and familiarity with him by the loftier kinds of meditation." Judging therefore by the criterion of virtues or by their fruits, it appears that spiritual contemplatives can often attain a greater union with God than the mystic. However, the opposite can also be true.

Union with God depends on the degree of one's charity which in its turn depends upon the degree of one's faith. Let us first consider faith. Both mystical and spiritual contemplatives must live by faith; but can we say which has the greater faith? The mystic certainly has a greater experience of faith; but is it greater for that reason? Charity and faith are tested not by one's consolations but by what he is willing to suffer and endure. He who can persevere in faith with fewer consolations would seem to have the greater faith, which seems more true of the spiritual contemplative. However, although the mystic has greater consolations, he generally has greater trials as well, and so we cannot really judge.

We can also consider the roots or source of one's faith, according to those words of our Lord, "More blessed are they who have not seen and have believed." It has also been aptly said, "The faith of those who believe because they have seen a miracle has no roots within themselves ... another miracle might efface it; the faith of those who believe without having seen has its roots within themselves in their free will." Does the faith of the mystic spring more from the experiences he has received, or from the inner strength of his will? Since the spiritual contemplative has nothing else but his will to base his faith on, his faith can only come from within and so it could be greater.

What has been said of faith equally applies to charity. Charity is not to be judged by the consolations one receives, but by the suffering and trials he is willing to endure for the beloved. Thus, charity also is greater when it springs more from within the soul, from one's free will. Is not this perhaps why God seems so sparing with his grace? In his desire to save all men, God could give efficacious grace to everyone, for it is certainly within his power to so reveal his goodness that one could not do otherwise than freely love him. That he does not do so, but rather sends us many trials which make it very difficult for us to see and understand his love, can only be because he knows that the degree of our union with him depends on the charity that comes from within and not from without. Since spiritual contemplatives receive fewer consolations, it would seem that their charity must come more from within and so could be greater.

When one reads of the powerful effects certain mystical experiences can produce in the soul, it would seem that they are the greatest source of santification. Thus, St. Teresa has said that God can do in one moment what the soul could not do in ten years. That, no doubt, is true; but it would seem that God could also do just as much in a soul through some trial, and so we cannot really judge.

In contemplation the soul is passive, and this is true of both the mystic and the spiritual contemplative. However, this passivity differs even as the passivity of a horse to man may differ. In mystical contemplation God, by his absolute power, simply carries us to where he wants us to go, as a man might transport a horse, and we need do nothing but simply consent and accept to be carried. This is certainly a wonderful and quite extraordinary manifestation of God's supreme dominion and power, a kind of miracle. In spiritual contemplation, however, God simply guides us, as a rider guides a horse, but we must use our own God-given powers to come to the goal to which God is guiding us. This is certainly a more natural and normal way and hence much more in accord with God's ordinary way of leading us. For this reason it would seem we should expect spiritual contemplation to be the more general way by which God leads men to perfection, and mystical contemplation the exception.

Conclusion

Let us recall that since contemplation consists in recognizing and accepting our relationship of dependence upon God who calls us to share in his divine life, it is something to which all Christians and even all men are called. Hence, it is in the ordinary way of the spiritual life. Also, since supernatural contemplation rests on faith, it cannot exist without experiencing the passive purgations in some form, for only in this way can we come to accept the reality of faith that our salvation is God's gift and not our own doing.

It should be clear that there are two ways by which God leads souls to union with himself and that he chooses the way he knows to be the best for each person. We should then be perfectly content with the way God has chosen for us and not go hankering after something which we may think is more perfect in itself, but to which God has not called us. Mystical contemplation is indeed a desirable good, but being overly concerned about obtaining it could be an imperfection in love; one can be seeking therein an experience of God rather than God himself. When we remember how St. John of the Cross insists on the necessity of living by faith alone and that one must place no value on mystical experiences, we wonder how perfection ever became so linked with the mystical state. What makes mystical contemplation sanctifying is the same as that which makes spiritual contemplation sanctifying: accepting and living the faith working through charity. Whether faith is experienced in one way rather than in another is not of any essential importance.

We can now see why mystical contemplation is a free gift of God which cannot be merited. If it were in the ordinary way of the spiritual life, then all should be able to obtain it through the ordinary means of grace. However, it is a free gift which God gives as he sees best for his own plans. Hence, its possession in no way proves that one has been more faithful or more generous.

God calls us to friendship, to a union of love with himself, wherein his will becomes our will and our will in some ineffable way becomes his will; we become one with him in his divine life. When we arrive at this point in the spiritual life we can cry out with St. Paul, "I live, now not I, but Christ lives in me," or in the words of St. John of the Cross we can say, "I shall see you in your beauty and you will see me in your beauty and I shall see myself in you, in your beauty; and you will see yourself in me in your beauty. . . . And thus I shall be you in your beauty and you will be me in your beauty, because your beauty itself will be my beauty and thus we shall see each other in your beauty. This is the adoption of the sons of God, who will truly say to God that which the Son himself said through St. John to the Eternal Father: 'All my things are Thine and Thy things are mine.' "